the geek handbook

Practical Skills
and Advice for
the Likeable
Modern Geek

Alex Langley

Published by

Krause Publications, a division of F+W Media, Inc.
700 East State Street • Iola, WI 54990-0001
715-445-2214 • 888-457-2873
www.krausebooks.com

To order books or other products call toll-free 1-800-258-0929
or visit us online at www.krausebooks.com

Front photo: Beloved geek Sheldon Cooper (Jim Parsons) from *The Big Bang Theory*. Copyright CBS Photo Archives/Getty Images.

ISBN-13: 978-1-4402-3288-6
ISBN-10: 1-4402-3288-1

Cover Design by Sharon Bartsch
Designed by Jana Tappa
Edited by Kristine Manty

Printed in USA

To Dad, for planning the heist.
To Katrina, for knocking out the guards.
To Nicholas, for snatching the loot.
And to Mom, for driving the getaway car.

Special Thanks

First of all I'd like to thank Dr. Andrea Letamendi, Manuel Yoro, Audrey Manning, KC Green, and Kimmie Britt for contributing their geeky experiences to the book.

I'd also like to thank the North Branch Writer's Critique Group for helping me sharpen my skills. Without you guys, I'd still be angrily punching out sentence fragments at my keyboard like a chimpanzee driven berserk by a complicated math problem.

Thanks to the OC Remix community for giving me such amazing music to listen to while working on my many, many projects.

Thanks to my grandparents, who have always believed in and supported me, the rest of my family, and all of my great friends over the years who've helped keep me laughing and keep me going. You guys know who you are.

Thanks to the following guys who have inspired me to try to write, think, and be funny since a young age: Bill Murray, "Weird" Al Yankovic, Gary Larson, Bill Watterson, Joss Whedon, and Terry Pratchett.

contents

7 | INTRODUCTION—HOW TO GEEK IT UP LIKE A G

11: Geek History: It's All Geek to Me

16 | CHAPTER ONE—KNOW YOUR GEEKS

28 | CHAPTER TWO—GEEK FASHION: Lose the Ponytail, You're Not the Friggin' Highlan

30: Things You Should Never Ever Wear

31: Things You Should Only Sometimes Wear

32: Things You Should Consider Wearing More Often

33: Tips for Keeping Your Geeky Self Groomed

35: Hairstyles: If We Were Hairless, We'd Look Like Big Thumbs

42 | CHAPTER THREE—HOW TO MAKE FRIENDS AND INFLUENCE GEEKS:
Tips on Interacting with Other People

46: Reading Body Language: Like ESP, Only Real

50: Top Ten Geeky Social No-Nos

52: How to be Hospitable (Without Being Too Hospitable)

54: Top Five Ways of Making Your Guests Feel Welcome

55: Just Say No: Letting Your Guests Know When It's Time to Get the Hell Out

56: How to Deal With Uncomfortable Situations

60: Top Fifteen Geek Greetings

64 | CHAPTER FOUR—GEEKTIVITIES: So You've Got Some Friends. What Now?

66: Multiplayer Games More Inescapably Addictive than the Madness of Cthulhu

67: So Bad They're Good

70: Tabletop Gaming: Rollin' on Twenties

72: Twelve Types of People You'll See at a Dungeons and Dragons Game

78 | CHAPTER FIVE—GETTING TO KNOW GEEK CULTURE, FUTURE AND PAST

80: We've Changed History: Ten Franchises that Forever Altered the Landscape of Geek Culture

89: Webcomics: Like Regular Comics, Only Webbier

95: The Top 10 Worst Moments in DC and Marvel Comics History

99: The Bizarre Superhero and Supervillain Bazaar

108 | CHAPTER SIX—GEEKERCISE: How to Break a Sweat Without Breaking Your Ankle

114 | CHAPTER SEVEN—GEEK TECH: Over 9,000 Gadgets You Can Waste Money On
116: Top Ten Home Appliances Most Likely to Kill You Once Machines Become Self-Aware
   (And How They'll Probably Do It)
118: Top Five Games to Play While Listening to Boring Speeches During Graduation
118: Fifteen Futuristic Inventions We Should Have By Now But Don't
119: Ten of the Goofiest Things Ever Invented

122 | CHAPTER EIGHT—THE INTERNET: Bringing Geeks Together
Since Al Gore Built It Out of a Series of Tubes
127: The Internet Commenter Zodiac
132: Choosing a Computer That's Right For You

134 | CHAPTER NINE—EDUCATION: Becoming the Big Geek on Campus
137: Popular Geeky Majors
138: Ten Ways to Get the Most Out of College Without Getting Expelled
   Due to *Animal House*-style Shenanigans
140: Collegiate Secret Societies Secretive Enough to be Cool
   But Not So Secretive We Don't Know About Them
141: Six Schools You Should Think Twice About
143: Top Three Worst High Schools in the Nation

144 | CHAPTER TEN—GEEKS IN THE WORKPLACE
146: The Top Six Greatest Geeky Professions
147: Jobs That Might Seem Like a Perfect Fit For Geeks
   But Aren't All They're Cracked Up To Be
148: How to Subtly Show Off Your Geekiness at Non-Geeky Jobs

152 | CHAPTER ELEVEN—THE HOUSE ENERGON BUILT: Maintaining a Geeky Home
154: Types of Homes and How Well They Fare Against Zombies
157: A Quick and Dirty Zombie Defense Guide
161: Living with Others: How to Get Along and Not Act Like the Cast of The Real World
161: Tips for Proper Roommate Etiquette
164: The Seven Types of Geek Roommates
166: Pets, Our Fuzzy Freeloaders
170: Cleanliness: It's the Latest Thing
172: How to Manage Your Hard-Earned Space Bucks: Geeking Out on a Budget

174 | CHAPTER TWELVE—WITH GREAT GEEKDOM COMES GREAT RESPONSIBILITY: Doing Good as a Geek

178 | CHAPTER THIRTEEN—GEEK COOKING: Using Your Bat'leth to Prepare Thanksgiving Dinne

180: Fighting Back Your Dark Hunger: Cooking It Old School

182: Recipes: You've Gotta Do the Cooking by the Book

185: Nutrition: Get You Some!

186 | CHAPTER FOURTEEN—BOLDLY GO WHERE LOTS OF PEOPLE HAVE GONE BEFORE: The Best Places for Geeks to Visit

188: Top Five Geeky Vacation Spots

189: Home is Where the Hulk is: Top Five Conventions Geeks Must Attend

190: The Handy Convention Survival Guide

195: Top Five Sexiest Characters to Cosplay

196: For the Hoard: What to Do With All That Treasure

198 | CHAPTER FIFTEEN—GEEK GIRLS: The Female is the Deadlier of the Species

200: History of the Geek Girl

201: Geek Guys: How to Not Feel So Weird Around Girls

202: Geek Girls: How to Deal With Those Silly Boys

203: Girl vs. Girl: When the Controllers are Down, the Adamantium Claws Come Out

205: Ladies Who Set a Good Example

207: Fiction's Most Badass Action Chicks

212 | CHAPTER SIXTEEN—GEEK LOVE: The Fifth Element

214: Ways to Have Fun While Dating and Not Accidentally End Up On a Date With a Person Who is Secretly an Evil Robot or Something

216: Top Five Reasons It's Better to Date Geeks

218: Tips for Dating a Geek

219: Oddball Fetishes Geek Culture has Propagated

222: Throwing a Geeky Bachelor/Bachelorette Party

224: The Top Five Best Geeky Wedding Themes

228 | CHAPTER SEVENTEEN—RAISING THEM RIGHT: How to Forge Little Geeks Your Own

230: Top Ten Most Popular Baby Geek Names

231: Geek Rites of Passage

235: The Future of Geekdom: Why It's a Good Day to Roll the Die

236 | INDEX

239 | ABOUT THE AUTHOR AND ILLUSTRATOR

introduction

how to geek it up
like a G

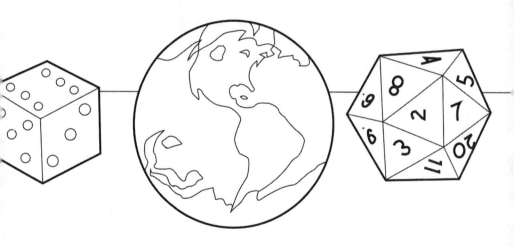

"The geek shall inherit the Earth."
— Source unknown, but he or she was probably super cool.

I've got news for you: the geeks *have* inherited the Earth. Just look around. Geek is chic, it's now, it's *it,* baby. Every year, superhero films pull in billions upon billions of dollars. The video game industry annually rakes in around 40 *billion* dollars.[1] Some of the top-rated television shows in recent history include one about a group of geeky physicists and engineers dealing with their hot blonde neighbor (*The Big Bang Theory*), another about people being lost on a time-traveling island (*Lost*), and a program about a doctor who travels through time and space kicking the ass of every evil alien hell-bent on conquering Earth (*Dr. Who*). There's a reason geek culture is dominating pop culture right now: it's freaking awesome!

But what about the time spent outside of geekiness, the space between the panels? For many, this non-geek time feels dreary, like traveling from a world of color back into a world of black and white; from gourmet meals to mouthfuls of sand; from floating peacefully in a river to getting creepy massages from Ramon, He Who Stares Too Much And Lives Down the Hall. Those are extreme examples, of course, but the point is that when geeks aren't enveloped in the safety of the things they love is when things often become confusing, stilted even. However, it doesn't have to be that way. There's a lot to life outside of watching TV, reading comic books, and playing video games, and this handbook is here to show you how great those other things can be.

So think of this handbook as two things: a handbook on going through your daily life with a geeky flair, as well as a celebration of all things geek. In some ways, this guidebook is the *itgetsbetter.org* of geek culture, filled with anecdotes from successful geeks from all walks of life to help closeted geeks know you should embrace who you are, because who you are is awesome. In other ways, it's a guide to doing things *our* way—the geek way. Things like:

• Getting a job that won't make you feel like a mindless cog in the machine.
• How to take soul-sucking jobs and transmogrify them into something fun.
• Five warning signs your Roomba might secretly be plotting against you.
• Romance. To woo, or not to woo? That is the question.

---

[1] To put that in perspective, that's enough money to buy every single car in every single car dealership in your hometown, fill them all with gold-covered toilets, and train an elite team of baboons to race across America while transporting said gold toilets and still have a few bucks left over for a flat screen TV.

- Basics on social interaction, both online and off, and how to troll like a gentleman (or gentlelady).
- Fashion. Just because you *can* wear socks with sandals doesn't mean you *should.*
- Making friends.
- Making dinner.
- Making babies.
- Geeky charities that give you a +1 to your Light Side score and a warm feeling in your tummy.
- The long, rich history of geekdom, extending all the way back to the first cave-geek in prehistoric times.
- Geek girls: tips on interacting with or becoming one of these burgeoning beauties.

Maybe you're a newbie geek living on your own for the first time. Or perhaps you're an experienced geek who desires some tips about hot human-on-human interaction. You could even be a geek-in-training who wants to learn a little bit more about the culture before joining it, in much the same way you should learn some Spanish before visiting Mexico, otherwise you may have to hurriedly mime "bathroom" to a Mexican gas station attendant while hoping to God your bowels don't burst. Regardless of your level of geekdom, we've got you covered. You see, there's a unique art to geekiness, and this book is here to exhibit that art with pride.

"In the sweet spot, right there in the middle, is the tripartite synergy that creates the geek. The mixture of knowledge (about comic books, particle physics, or the works of Mozart), obsessiveness (they'll sit in front of a computer or a workbench for hours perfecting, building, or playing anything), and social skills (they actually get together with people for pen-and-paper RPGs or get in line with a bunch of friends to see the midnight showing of the next *Star Trek* movie), that makes a well-rounded, self-sustaining person of affable oddity."
— Ken Denmead, engineer, author, and editor
of Wired.com's GeekDad blog

Super Cave Man

Geek History: It's All Geek to Me

The kingdom of geeks is a land with a rich and colorful history dating all the way back to the beginning of time. Whenever a Trekkie taps the communicator on his Starfleet uniform, he's actually tapping into an ancient heritage that can be traced back to the dawn of civilization. Don't believe me? Check out this very real account of geeks throughout time.

500,000 B.C. Neanderthal Ug-thag M'grog told the story of a caveman from a faraway cave who crash landed on Earth in a "sky log." This caveman was faster than a speeding dinosaur, more powerful than a wooly mammoth, and could leap tall volcanoes in a single bound.

2300 B.C. Noah got sick of two geeks sniggering at the "Blue-footed Boobies" waddling around the ark and conked their heads together, making a coconut sound. The geeks then drew a series of drawings of Angry Man Noah highlighting how easily the bearded one gets angered, with each comic ending with Noah's catch phrase, "Noah no likeses!" These crude pictograms were the precursor to modern internet memes such as Rage Comics, Pokedads and Advice Dogs, and, much like modern memes, the Angry Man Noah jokes were copied and repeated until they reached critical levels of un-funniness.

1200 B.C. After accidentally resurrecting a frog through the use of a small lightning rod, a potato, and an electrical storm, Egyptian prince Nashtet became history's first mad scientist.

255 B.C. Archimedes laughed at a joke he found buried within a math formula. Thousands of years would pass before the rest of the Earth's mathematicians become advanced enough to understand what the heck Archimedes thought was so funny.

800 A.D. The Dark Ages were a bountiful time for geeks, as their proclivities toward staying indoors kept them away from most of the plagues ripping their way across the planet. As a result, geek numbers were thriving—until the church started hanging scientists, which pretty much sent geeks back to square one.

1488 A.D.	Leonardo Da Vinci, the world's first master of everything, created and invented everything from flying machines to submarines. He also invented the *dispositivo di controllo dell'anatra,* a device that let him control the thoughts of ducks. As a result, the feathery fowl were reduced from the mighty warrior beasts they once were into the docile creatures we know today.
1501 A.D.	To help pass the time between battles, a samurai fantasized about being a samurai with a really, *really* sharp sword, one that could cut through bad guys like a knife through butter. This story was passed down and modified from generation to generation until modern times, where it became known as the television show *Iron Chef.*
1620 A.D.	The pilgrims frowned heavily on any sort of geekery, encouraging their kids to do healthy things such as playing outside and burning witches.
1886 A.D.	Seconds after Winifred Edgerton became the first woman in the world to get a PhD, she became an Aphrodite to the geek community, her professional research rendered to a near standstill by the number of geeky guys clamoring to ask her out.
1890 A.D.	9:36 p.m. Louis Lumiere invented the first moving picture, the precursor to modern films.
1890 A.D.	9:37 p.m. Chas Moreau pirated the world's first movie when he sketched copies of Lumiere's first film and distributed them illegally to his friends.
1896 A.D.	Thomas Edison mooned Nikola Tesla, creating the world's first mad scientist rivalry. Their enmity toward one another would go unmatched until the famous 1996 case of *Dexter versus Mandark.*
1897 A.D.	Nikola Tesla invented a teleportation device. Thomas Edison called him a nerd and Tesla destroyed the machine in a fit of shame.
1901 A.D.	At the 1901 World's Fair, key speaker Nikola Tesla's perpetual energy device was upstaged by Edison's new invention, the Nipple Elongator.
1904 A.D.	Edison unleashed an army of mechanical crickets into Tesla's home, driving the man to near-madness by their incessant chirping.
1908 A.D.	Edison admitted he stole "more than a few" ideas from Tesla, followed up by stating he "couldn't give less of a damn about it."

1910 A.D.	Tesla got the last laugh on Edison by rounding up the mechanical crickets and teleporting them throughout space and time, following the man wherever he went to the end of his days. Edison's last words were: "Tesla! I'll get you if it's the last thing I-WILL SOMEONE SQUISH THAT GYAT-DANG CRICKET?!?"
1911 A.D.	Marie Curie was bitten by a radioactive spider and enjoyed a short-lived stint as the Amazing Spider-Curie.
1915 A.D.	The world's first film geek criticized *Birth of a Nation,* calling it "Really, really racist. Like, surprisingly so."

The Duck Army.

Edison vs. Nikola: The Mecha Crickets.

1916 A.D. The Typhoid Mary Fan Club finally got to meet its idol. The club disbanded a few months later, due to low membership.

1941 A.D. In a desperate bid to win World War II, Adolf Hitler had his top scientists create a genetically engineered superweapon. The result? Actor Don Knotts.

1950 A.D. During the "furious fifties," the American government gave millions of dollars to every crackpot with a PhD, resulting in the invention of: credit cards, super glue, power steering, Mr. Potato Head, huge radioactive grasshoppers, those little seeds on hamburger buns, hovercrafts, laser guns, spazer guns, and phazer guns.

1984 A.D. *Ghostbusters,* starring Bill "Don't Call Me Phil" Murray, Harold Ramis, Dan Akroyd, and Ernie Hudson, busted into theaters and the world became a better place.

1987 A.D. The modern Internet was invented and geeks worldwide breathed a collective sigh of relief as they realized going outside is a thing of the past.

1992 A.D. Genetically engineered killer tomatoes attacked France.

1998 A.D. Scientists activated The Large Hadron Collider, destroying and recreating the universe in an instant, with the only difference being that there are now 7 percent fewer clowns in all of space and time. Science then congratulated itself on what is arguably its greatest accomplishment.

2001 A.D. The proliferation of text messaging led to people texting while on the go, causing a 65 percent increase in toe-stubbing worldwide.

2002 A.D. *Spider-Man* swung into theaters, beginning the long reign of geek movies as cinema's most powerful force, solidifying into something so mighty that not even the awfulness of another *Batman & Robin* could stop it.

EARLY 2012 A.D. Astrophysicist Neil deGrasse Tyson's lecturing skills became so finely honed that he delivered a full day of powerpoint-based lectures while asleep.

LATE 2012 A.D. The dead rose from their graves to feast on the living, giving zombie apocalypse nuts something to feel excited about and Mayan calendar nuts something to feel smug about.

2013 A.D. Zombie apocalypse nuts thwart the undead uprising with relative ease, disappointing many.

know
your geeks

How to spot,
identify, and
even become a
real-live geek.

Much like ice cream and Christopher Walkens, geeks come in many different flavors. If you believe you or someone you love may be a geek, or are interested in becoming a geek yourself, thumb through the following list of the major geek subtypes to see if any of these traits sound familiar or pique your interest. Also know that a person is not limited to a single type of geekiness. In fact, many of these subtypes often go hand-in-hand with each other.

If you realize that you're one or more of these kinds of geeks, don't worry. It just means you're gonna know friggin' *everything* about that subject, giving you an honorary PhD in kickass-itude.[2]

---

[2] Also remember that these are rough guidelines as to what these types of geeks are like. The modern geek comes in many forms, and these simple caricatures of them are to educate and amuse, not to put down. So if it seems like I'm making fun of a type of geek, I'm really not. Hell, I fit most of these categories myself, anyway.

Tabletop Geek

Some say the tabletop geek is truly the first geek, that cavegeeks were playing games of *Tunnels and Tyrannosaurs* with crude dice carved from the bones of a saber tooth tiger and colored with the feces of a wooly mammoth.

ACTIVITY OF CHOICE: Any game that requires a table or some sort of flat surface to play, such as *Dungeons and Dragons, Warhammer,* or *Don't Let the Gnomes Poot in Your Lap!*

APPEARANCE: The easiest way to spot a tabletop gamer is to look for two key signs: a Crown Royal bag for holding their dice, or brushes and small containers of paint used to color their army of choice. Be warned, though, that the latter is easily confused for an art major. A quick questionnaire about vector-based imaging and which *Warhammer* race is the most overpowered will let you know whether you've got an art or a tabletop geek on your hands.

LOCATION OF CHOICE: Anywhere with a flat surface. Some of the less intelligent tabletop geeks may attempt to use walls as their playing surface, which won't work because of, well, gravity and stuff.

HOW TO BECOME ONE: Tabletop gaming isn't something you can do by yourself, so if you don't know anyone else who is already into the hobby, you'll have to find someone who is. I'd recommend hanging around your local comics/tabletop gaming store. If you're poorly versed in the way of the D20, they'll probably be more than happy to educate you, and from there you can decide which games you enjoy and don't, as well as finding a few players with which to form your own gaming group.

History Geek

Master of the history book, a history geek's job is to know everything that's ever happened, no matter how insignificantly esoteric it may be.

ACTIVITY OF CHOICE: Reading about wars, famine, plagues ... you know, fun stuff.

APPEARANCE: Khakis, fuzzy sweaters, and pretty much anything brown.

LOCATION OF CHOICE: The library.

NOTE: Watch out if a history geek gets her hands on a time machine, as she may travel back in time in an attempt to see history firsthand. You'll know this has happened if you stumble across a woodcarving that looks suspiciously familiar.

HOW TO BECOME ONE: If you find yourself interested in history enough to surround yourself with moldy books and other historically like-minded individuals, you might have what it takes to become a history geek. If you're looking for points in history to begin studying, I'd recommend U.S. history, particularly focusing on the "big five" for the U.S.— World War I and II, the Revolutionary War, pretty much all of the sixties, and the *Star Wars* Christmas Special. After that, everything else is just fudge on the historical sundae.

Sci-fi Geek

Have you ever seen the special director's cut edition of *Blade Runner*, the one where Harrison Ford's been digitally replaced by Danny Glover and Mel Gibson? The sci-fi geek has, and she loves it. It may not be as good as the Super Special Ultra Extended Director's Cut II Turbo Edition, but it's not bad if you don't know any better. Sci-fi geeks eat up science fiction films, books, and TV shows at a ravenous pace, consuming 2.92^{X874} pieces of media per hour.

ACTIVITY OF CHOICE: Reading or watching anything sci-fi, or anything with Nathan Fillion in it.

LOCATION OF CHOICE: At home, buried in either a book, television screen, or computer monitor.

NOTE: Sci-fi geeks can occasionally get it in their heads that they're going to invent the next great piece of future tech. Sometimes this leads to them accidentally losing a finger or two to a homemade lightsaber, while other times it leads to them getting a PhD in physics. Either way, it's best to keep a close eye on them.

HOW TO BECOME ONE: There are a number of movies and TV shows that any sci-fi geek worth his or her salt has seen, including (but not limited to): *Blade Runner*, the *Star Wars* trilogy (the original, not the prequels you plebian cur), any and all *Star Trek*, *Doctor Who*, and *Hercules vs. Karate*.

Sports Geek

You know those guys who paint their faces at football games? That's cosplay, people. Geekery is defined by an obsessive knowledge of a subject, and two guys who are arguing whether the '85 Bears could have taken on the '62 Packers are just as geeky as the guys debating who would win in a fight, Batman or Superman.[3]

ACTIVITY OF CHOICE: Tailgating, watching the pre-pre-pregame, or sitting at the computer putting together the perfect roster for his fantasy football team.

APPEARANCE: His favorite team's jersey or face paint to help support the team and belly paint to shame his family.

---

[3] If there's ever a debate as to who will win in a fight between Batman and anyone else, the answer is always Batman.

LOCATION OF CHOICE: Wherever there's beer and balls.

NOTE: Sometimes the sports geek will lapse into a state of utter sadness, convinced that he could've gone pro, if only the coach had put him in during that key game, or if he hadn't blown out his knee junior year, or if he had any talent at football. When this happens, try to distract the sports geek with beer and a copy of the 1992 VHS *Slam Jam Masters—Dunks U Won't Believe!*

HOW TO BECOME ONE: Choose a sport, or multiple sports, that you enjoy watching. View enough games and learn enough about the players to construct a fantasy football/basketball/Calvinball team. Once you have finished your first fantasy league team, your transformation will be complete. Wait two to four weeks for the arrival of a complimentary package consisting of your team's jersey and a can of body paint color-coded to match the jersey.

Music Geek

The music geek's favorite band is *Clandestine Dandelions*. You haven't heard of them? She's not surprised; they're pretty underground. *So* underground, in fact, that she's the only person who has ever heard of *Clandestine Dandelions* because it's *her* one-woman band and she's refused to ever perform in front of anyone else because they won't "get it."

ACTIVITY OF CHOICE: Listening to music. The fewer people who have heard of it, the better.

APPEARANCE: Headphones, out of date hats, scarves when it's warm, women's jackets (on men), fake mustaches (on women), pants that are tight in unflattering ways, and ironic T-shirts for '80s children's shows.

LOCATION OF CHOICE: Concerts, record stores, and coffee houses.

NOTE: There are two subtypes of music geeks: hipsters and musicians. Hipsters are creatures with the aforementioned qualities of loving only that which is ironic and underground. Musicians are people with enough love of music to actually pursue it for a living, and often have enough musical knowledge and talent to make hipsters wither and die in their presence. In the event of cross-pollination between the two groups, you will come out with someone who is not only insufferably smug, but unbelievably talented, meaning you and everyone around them will likely hate how much they love their music.

HOW TO BECOME ONE: Both listening to and learning how to play an instrument are good starts to becoming a music geek. The guitar is often the instrument of choice for self-learners, as it's easy to carry, sexy-looking, and there are plenty of instructional videos on Youtube that can teach you how to play. Youtube is honestly a great starting point for wannabe music geeks. Find as many bands as you can and listen to them all, making sure to take note of both the popular and relatively unknown ones, so you can appear both educated on what's hip, as well as knowledgeable on the underground music scene.

Comic Book Geek

Before Hugh Jackman was filling movie screens with his handsome mug, the character Wolverine was first introduced in *The Incredible Hulk* #181, not in any *X-Men* comic. Many people will read that sentence and think, "Huh. That's interesting." A comic book geek, however, will read that and not only already know that, but they will have corrected the sentence by adding, " ... and while that issue is credited as his first appearance, *technically* he was first introduced on the last page of *The Incredible Hulk* #180."

ACTIVITY OF CHOICE: Reading comic books, watching comic book movies, and arguing whether DC or Marvel have lost their minds with their latest retcons.

APPEARANCE: Thanks to the spread of superheroes as a moneymaking force, comic book geeks have a wide variety of appearances. Those with a lust for flashiness will often wear shirts featuring huge collections of entire superhero teams. Those who prefer subtlety may be content to wear T-shirts with just a superhero's logo on it so only those in the know realize their geekiness. And those who aren't satisfied just reading the comics will often dress up as their favorite hero, mostly to cosplay and show off during conventions, but occasionally to fight crime.

LOCATION OF CHOICE: Comic book shops and conventions.

NOTE: If you're thinking of dressing up to fight crime, don't. We can't all be Spider-Man; it'd put Spidey out of a job.

HOW TO BECOME ONE: Read comic books. Continue reading them. Mission accomplished.

Gamer Geek

For the uninitiated, video games are simply movies that do what you want them to. For gamer geeks, however, video games are gateways into entirely new dimensions, filled with over-the-top heroics, monstrous foes, and brain-bending puzzles.

ACTIVITY OF CHOICE: Playing video games.

APPEARANCE: Glazed over expression due to frequent bouts of *Diablo III*-induced insomnia, sweatpants, and a hoody.

LOCATION OF CHOICE: In front of the TV/computer monitor.

NOTE: Feeding a gamer is a relatively easy task. Simply pour a Mountain Dew into his

mouth once in a while, throw in some Cheetos, and he will be good to go for another few hours. Hygiene, however, can be an issue. And don't be surprised if you find your gamer geek sitting atop a toilet, controller in hand, with his pants around his ankles, as he kills two birds with one flush.

HOW TO BECOME ONE: Much like being a Comic Book Geek, the requirements to be a Gamer Geek are fairly simple: play video games.

Automotive Geek

Cars. We all use them, but how many of us know how they work? While a car's inner functioning is still a mystery on par with Stonehenge or the brief popularity of *Jersey Shore*, there are those who excel in this arcane art and have familiarized themselves with the intricate bolts, nozzles, and doodads inside of a vehicle, and will gladly tell you the horsepower, torque, and vitality points of your engine. We call them ... auto geeks.

ACTIVITY OF CHOICE: Fixing up his car, washing/waxing his car, and, in extreme cases, making sweet, sweet love to his car.

APPEARANCE: Sweat on his brow, oil stains on his hand, and a picture of a '68 Firebird in his wallet.

LOCATION OF CHOICE: The garage/driveway.

NOTE: Collections are fine, in moderation. The automotive geek, however, will often try to collect cars, which is problematic due to three main factors:

1. Cars are expensive.

2. Cars take up a lot of space.

3. A car is, by nature, a pack-hunting predator, and will often attack their owner if their numbers reach great enough strength.

HOW TO BECOME ONE: Study up on what the little bells and doodads inside of your car are actually *for*. If you can remove anything from under the hood of your car, put it back and have it still function, then you've taken the first step toward becoming an automotive geek.

"Being a geek is all about being honest about what you enjoy and not being afraid to demonstrate that affection. It means never having to play it cool about how much you like something. It's basically a license to proudly emote on a somewhat childish level rather than behave like a supposed adult. Being a geek is extremely liberating."
— Simon Pegg, actor and writer

Anime Geek

Japan is a diverse land, filled with people as diverse as they are numerous. Their contributions to popular culture are just as varied, with one of the most global influences being anime. Anime are Japanese cartoons often featuring superpowered teens, ninjas, and panties. *Lots* of panties.

ACTIVITY OF CHOICE: Reading manga, watching anime, eating Pocky sticks, learning Japanese, and telling anyone who will listen about how they're moving to Japan as soon as they can get some money together.

APPEARANCE: Ponytail, shirts with dragons on them, shorts, socks, and sandals, backpacks in the shape of an anime's token cute creature character, katanas.

LOCATION OF CHOICE: Anime conventions, internet fansites, fan-fiction forums.

NOTE: Anime geeks may, on occasion, lose touch with reality and become convinced they are a character from their favorite cartoon. If this has happened to someone you know, visit www.myfriendthinksssheisananimecharacterandidon'tknowwhattodo.com. If this has happened to you, then the next time you leave this dimension to visit your superpowered friends, take me with you, because it sounds pretty sweet over there.

HOW TO BECOME ONE: Read up on Japanese culture. Watch an anime with its American dub and then watch it in Japanese with English subtitles to compare. Once you think the Japanese voice acting is superior to the English voice acting, or have purchased a body pillow/mousepad with boobs of an anime character, or have tried to cosplay as your favorite anime character, you can rest assured that you are now an Anime Geek.

Food Geek

We all have to eat, and while for many it's simply something to do in order to survive, for others the preparing and eating of food is an art unto itself.

ACTIVITY OF CHOICE: Oddly enough, food geeks spend far more time smelling food and talking about it than they do eating. It's almost as if they enjoy the thought of food more than the actual food itself.

APPEARANCE: A bottle of wine in hand and a pretentiously expensive chef's apron across her chest.

LOCATION OF CHOICE: The farmer's market searching for the best (probably organic) ingredients.

ALTERNATE NAME: Foodies.

HOW TO BECOME ONE: Being a food geek requires diligence, devotion, and deep pockets, as it generally requires you to study the reviews for every restaurant around and visit the highest rated ones, which are also coincidentally the priciest ones.

Tech Geek

The world must have tech geeks; while their obsession with technology will ultimately destroy them,[4] their technological brilliance improves the way we do everything.

ACTIVITY OF CHOICE: Taking things apart to figure out how they work, building their own laser beams, finding the end of the internet.[5]

APPEARANCE: Lack of fingerprints due to electrical burns, bracers to help ease the carpal tunnel they've obtained from spending twenty-two hours a day at the computer, four to five cell phones on their person at all times.

LOCATION OF CHOICE: The internet.

HOW TO BECOME ONE: Being a tech geek often leads to something called "Brand Loyalty," which means you will become fiercely devoted to a particular brand of technology to the point of looking down on people who don't have the brand you do—the "non-believers." It's not uncommon for tech geeks to challenge the non-believers to a few rounds in the Thunderdome, with the winner having to forfeit their brand and forever buy technology from the winner's company of choice. Microsoft didn't become a successful company due to its programs, it became a success because Bill Gates challenged people to Thunderdome matches like 24/7, and if there's one thing the dude's good at, it's beating asses in the Thunderdome.

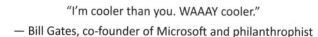

"I'm cooler than you. WAAAY cooler."
— Bill Gates, co-founder of Microsoft and philanthrophist

---

[4] 98 percent of all tech geeks die in technology related fatalities, including, but not limited to: crushed to death by iPad, computer virus, malevolent AI coming to life at just the wrong moment, electrical malfunction, and human/cyborg sexual relations.

[5] It's scary there. And the last guy is really hard to beat.

chapter two
geek
fashion:

**Lose the Ponytail—
You're Not the
Friggin' Highlander**

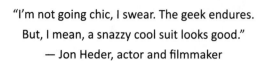

"I'm not going chic, I swear. The geek endures.
But, I mean, a snazzy cool suit looks good."
— Jon Heder, actor and filmmaker

F ashion is a common point of trouble to those of the geeky persuasion. Our idea of dressing up is often to put on a pair of dark socks to go with our sandals. But if you're looking to woo a new ladyfriend or gentleman, if you're at a school and looking to make some new buds, or if you just want to get a dang job, you'll want to dress to impress. Here are some common dos and don'ts every geek should know.

Things You Should Never *Ever* Wear

SOCKS AND SANDALS. Folks, socks and sandals look stupid. Extremely stupid. There is no condition in which they don't look stupid. If you are wearing socks, don't wear sandals. If you are wearing sandals, don't wear socks. If you are wearing both, remove one.

MUTTON CHOPS. The only person on whom mutton chops are an appropriate hairstyle is Mr. Hyde. Unless you are, in fact, the dark half of Dr. Jekyll, don't grow your sideburns into mutton chops.

UTILIKILTS. I've got news for you: when you're wearing a utilikilt, you're wearing a dress. I know they're functional and breezy, but so are shorts, and shorts have a much lower risk of having your testicles flop out for God and everyone to see.

CROCS. Crocs shoes look like regular shoes that have been the victim of a drive-by shooting. Put these poor shoes out of their misery by not wearing them.

CALCULATOR WATCHES. One part wristwatch. One part calculator. When added together, they create a fashion faux pas so powerful it will prevent anyone from ever wanting to touch you or your fun parts.

NECKBEARDS. When growing a beard, please make sure you can generate enough facial hair to cover the entire lower half of your face, cheek to cheek. Do not grow a beard that only covers your neck, as it makes most people look like goobers who don't know what a beard is. And if you can grow a full beard, either keep it trimmed or grow it to epic Dwarven proportions, anything in between may make you look like a hobo.

NECKBEARS. Bears for covering the neck with. Warm, but heavy, and really dangerous.

HEAVILY TORN CLOTHING. It's not the '90s anymore, and Kurt Cobain has been dead for a long, long time. Torn clothing should really only be worn if you're doing something really messy, such as painting a house or feeding spaghetti to a hippopotamus.

TOE SHOES. For those who don't know, toe shoes are those weird sneakers that have individual grooves for your toes, giving your feet the appearance of someone who's been stepping in fresh cement.

"I'm still a geek on the inside, that's the important thing."
— "Weird" Al Yankovic, geek music icon

Things You Should Only *Sometimes* Wear

PONYTAILS. Ponytails do look good on some people. They almost always look good on girls, for example. But for many geeky guys, ponytails are simply a way to let their hair grow to unruly (and often greasy) lengths and keep it out of their face. Unless you're as manly or square-jawed of a man as Adrian "There Can Be Only One" Paul, a ponytail is probably not suited to the shape of your head. In all likelihood, having a ponytail will make you look like a human rat or a pre-fat Steven Seagal, neither of which are good things.

FEDORAS. Fedoras can be one of the most stylish things a person can wear. They're sleek, they're stylish, and there's a reason pretty much everyone on *Mad Men* wears one. But if you wear one with your Iron Man T-shirt, it makes you look incapable of dressing yourself. If you're going to wear a fedora, dress in equally nice clothing, and make sure everything fits.

BOWTIES. Bowties almost always look out of place, with the primary exception being Doctor Who cosplay. Then bowties are cool.

STEAMPUNK. While fun and whimsical, steampunk is best in moderation, and most appropriate in any place where you'd find cosplay. Also, try to use the correct type of materials when constructing your steampunk outfit. There's nothing sadder than a steampunk soldier in polyester pants holding a Styrofoam gun with a clock and gears drawn on it in magic marker.

COSPLAY. It's okay to cosplay at Comic-Con, the world's largest comic-book convention. It's not okay to cosplay at Gramma's funeral.

RETRO CLOTHES. Wearing throwback T-shirts from the extreme '90s is fun and awesome ... to a point. But your *California Dreams* T-shirt isn't going to be nearly as funny when your friends see you wearing it three times a week.

SWEATPANTS. Sweatpants are great to wear to the gym, or around the house, or for quick late night trips to Taco Bell. But wearing them out during the day isn't a great way to impress other people, as they'll see you and likely think, "What a slob." Try to keep it to things like jeans, khakis, skirts ... anything that doesn't make you look like Carl from *Aqua Teen Hunger Force*.[6]

---

[6] The only exception to this are guys who are so well endowed that sweatpants are pretty much the only pants that fit them comfortably, or people who are getting laid so much that pants are almost an afterthought. However, unless you're Jason Stackhouse, you may not need to worry about such things, and if you are Jason Stackhouse, I feel it's my duty to let you know that your sister has porked a lot of vampires.

LEATHER JACKETS. There's a thin line between a leather jacket making you look cool and just making you *think* you look cool. Before you buy one, consult a few of your more fashionable (and objective) friends.

DARK SHIRTS. Next time you're at a convention, or are looking through pictures of people at conventions, check out the color of every shirt around. Odds are they're black. Geeks wear black because it makes us look thinner, dapper, and less sweaty, which is great. But a cleverly applied blue shirt can help you stand out from a sea of black-shirted badasses.

COLOGNE/PERFUME. When putting on cologne, you should, and I cannot emphasize this enough, apply it in MODERATION FOR FRAK'S SAKE. How many times have you been in an elevator with some guy so overly cologned it's as if he's deployed a bio-weapon en route to the 15th floor? A light spritz is enough to get you smelling nice, folks. What you should not do, however, is forego bathing in favor of taking an Axe bath, which is where you spray yourself with enough Axe bodyspray to choke a donkey.[7]

T-SHIRTS WITH HUGE PICTURES OF DRAGONS OR SUPERHERO TEAMS. These kinds of images make great wallpapers for your computer but don't always translate as well when plastered across a human body.

Things You Should Consider Wearing *More* Often

A CLEAN-SHAVEN FACE. All too often you'll see geeks who forego shaving in favor of growing goatees so haggard it looks as if they were eating a squirrel and stopped as they reached the tail.

NAIL POLISH. While this tip is mostly directed at the ladies, any guys who are deep into the alt/hipster/dubstep/dookiestep scenes are often encouraged to throw some color onto their fingertips, too. Just pick a color other than black, okay? Black is so 1998.

SIZE APPROPRIATE CLOTHING. Far too many geeks wear clothes that are too big, making them look like a kid playing dress up in Dad's clothes, or clothes that are too small, making them look like the Hulk mid-transformation.

BLAZERS. A good blazer can be your best friend. Not in the literal sense, of course, unless you own some kind of special Narnian blazer that gives you advice when you need it most. But as a fashion item, a blazer can be combined with a nice shirt and jeans for a slick look when out on the town, or a dress shirt/pants if you're applying for a job or

---

[7] Once, while I was riding a school bus, a kid in the back sprayed so much bodyspray on himself that it set off the fire alarm and the bus had to pull over so the driver could inspect what the hell was happening. Everyone laughed, and the kid angrily threw his bodyspray out the window for embarrassing him. Don't be that kid.

trying to convince people you're Barney Stinson.

THE CONFIDENCE CLAUSE. Ultimately, what looks best on you is whatever you feel most confident in. If you like your utilikilt and feel proud of it, *wear* it. Don't let this list or any other control you.

Tips for Keeping Your Geeky Self Groomed

While geeks are fun and smart, we can, on occasion, be less than thoughtful when it comes to matters of personal hygiene. No one's judging, because surely *you're* not one of those hygiene-challenged geeks. But no matter the case, you should probably read this list of grooming tips. You know, so I don't feel like I've wasted my time writing them. You're doing me a service, if you think about it.

1. **DEODORANT: IT'S NOT A SUGGESTION.** Just because you don't think you stink doesn't mean you aren't stinky. We live in an enlightened, modern society filled with wondrous gadgets and inventions. The most important of these inventions is deodorant. Wearing deodorant is *never* a bad thing, and sometimes we geeks can get so excited about the release of a new game or about attending every single awesome panel at a convention that we forget that there are other people around, and that they can smell us.

2. **COMB YOUR HAIR.** The "I just rolled out of bed" look only works when you spend a half hour applying the right combination of holding gel and gentle teasing to your hair. If you go around looking as if you *really* just rolled out of bed, people are likely to confuse you for a homeless person, or a bear. Or a homeless bear.

3. **BRUSH YOUR TEETH.** Brush them when you wake up, before you go to bed, and anytime in between, especially if you eat anything particularly gritty or odiferous. Pop quiz: You finished chowing down on a massive pile of garlic bread right before hanging out in your friend's small apartment. Should you brush your teeth? Answer: YES. Question two: You've been chewing mint gum all day and now you're ready to go to bed. Should you brush your teeth? Answer: YES. Question three: A rabid badger has taken up residence in your bathroom so he can cry about his bad break-up

with Cindy the squirrel. Should you brush your teeth? Answer: Maybe, but only if you can talk the badger out peacefully without getting mauled. If mauling seems likely, it's better to let your dental hygiene take a hit for one night.

4. **IF YOU CAN'T GROW A FULL BEARD OR MANLY STUBBLE, SHAVE YOUR FACE.** Peach fuzz impresses no one.

5. **PASSING GAS IS NOT A SPORT.**[8] If you have to let one rip, do it quietly and preferably not in a crowded, enclosed space. If you find yourself in one of those places, do everyone around you a favor and step out for a second.

6. **IF YOU ARE A GIRL AND PLAN TO WEAR SHORTS AND/OR A TANK TOP, SHAVE YOUR LEGS AND PITS.** While there are a number of guys and girls who find a hairy lady attractive, they are few and far between. Most people will simply find a hirsute-pitted gal to be yucky.

7. **SHOWER FREQUENTLY.** Did you work outside today? Did you sweat at all? Did you stay up all night watching video remixes of Nyan Cat attacking the Star Wars Kid? If you answered yes to any of these questions, then it is in your best interest to take a shower. And, to those select few who argue that human hair is self-cleaning, I say you this: shut up and wash your greasy-ass hair. And your greasy ass hair.

8. **MAKE REGULAR TRIPS TO THE DENTIST AND DOCTOR.** Fact: Women tend to live longer than men. Why? Well, for one thing, you don't see videos of women saying things like, "Hi. I'm Joanna Knoxville and this is *Kicked in the Vulva by a Mule*." When you get a group of women together, they hang out. When you get a group of dudes together, they often do really, *really* stupid stuff because "It's awesome." And while, yes, it is awesome, it can also kill you. But the other, more important reason that women often live longer is because they make regular visits to the doctor and dentist, who will point out medical and dental issues well before they become full-blown problems. Men will often think, "Well, if it's gonna kill me, there ain't nothing that can be done about it. If it ain't gonna kill me, I don't need to visit anyway." *Wrong.* There's a third group of medical issues called "things that will become bigger problems without medical attention." So go to the friggin' doctor. If you're sick or injured and the thought ever crosses your mind that maybe you need to visit the hospital, just do it. Yes, it sucks to pay for your medical bills with the money you'd been saving to buy a life-sized Gundam, but it's better to be safe than to lose a toe to gangrene.

---

[8] Except in Mexico, where noble Fartadores will wrestle each other to the ground and fart in each other's faces for honor.

Hairstyles: If We Were Hairless, We'd Look Like Big Thumbs

Fictional characters have it easy. They look good in hideous spandex costumes, don't have to worry about paying rent, and their hairstyles can defy physics and God himself. There are a number of fictional characters with breath-takingly awesome hairdos, some of which are possible for us mere mortals to copy, while others make us appear stupendously doofy. Now, as a geek, you may be tempted to copy the look of your favorite hero. This can be a dangerous affair, as you don't have the advantage of a skilled artist making you look cool in every panel. Before you decide on which heroic haircut you're going for, why don't you take a step back and consider how they'd look in real life.

1. The Wolverine

COMPLEXITY: High

COOLNESS IF DONE RIGHT: Medium

LIKELIHOOD YOU'LL LOOK LIKE A JACKASS: Very high

Let's face it: while Wolverine may be one of the coolest mofos to ever walk the Earth, his choice of hairstyle is ... odd, at best. At worst, he looks like he's been caught in a wind tunnel while wearing a trucker cap. You'd be better off leaving this look to Hugh Jackman.

The Wolverine

2. The Tony Stark

COMPLEXITY: Low

COOLNESS IF DONE RIGHT: High

LIKELIHOOD YOU'LL LOOK LIKE A JACKASS: Low

The goatee plus short hair is a power look that never goes out of style. And remember, folks, it's 2012. Goatees aren't just for evil twins and Hans Gruber anymore. If you're looking to change your appearance, The Tony Stark is an easy fix. Just keep your hair short or you'll risk falling into the dreaded Simpsons' Comic Book Guy territory.

The Tony Stark

3. The Rogue

COMPLEXITY: Low

COOLNESS IF DONE RIGHT: Medium-high

LIKELIHOOD YOU'LL LOOK LIKE A JACKASS: Medium-low

Step 1: Dye a streak of hair white.

There is no step 2.

The Rogue is a simple look, providing an easy way to spice up your appearance without having to commit to anything drastic, such as costly extensions, or braids so tightly wound you feel like your eyeballs are going to explode. For added variety, you can dye the streak different colors, but don't over-dye that one strip of hair or you'll end up with locks so "frazzled," you'll appear to have a wad of cotton balls stuck to your forehead.

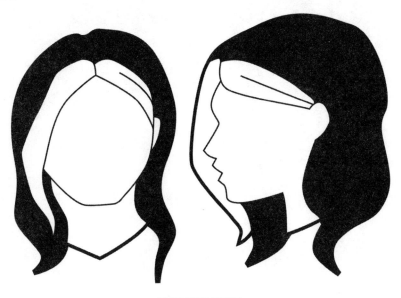

The Rogue

4. The Catwoman

COMPLEXITY: Medium

COOLNESS IF DONE RIGHT: High

LIKELIHOOD YOU'LL LOOK LIKE A JACKASS: High

Modern Catwoman's short-haired 'do can be a difficult look to pull off. Leave your hair too long and no one will notice. Cut it too short and you'll look like Felicity from the *bad* years. The Catwoman is a look that should be tested out with a series of progressively shorter haircuts; that way, if you ever find you've hit a haircut outside of your comfort zone, you'll only be a little outside of it instead of clear in another county.

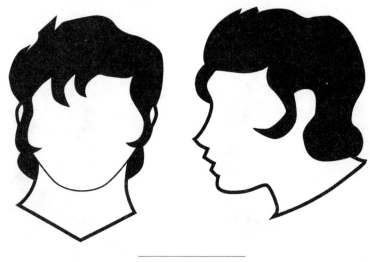

The Catwoman

5. The Cloud

COMPLEXITY: Very high

COOLNESS IF DONE RIGHT: High

LIKELIHOOD YOU'LL LOOK LIKE A JACKASS: High

For someone as generally apathetic as *Final Fantasy VII*'s Cloud Strife, the guy sure does put a lot of effort into his hair. He probably spends hours every day applying just the right combination of wax, hairspray, and heat to get it to stand up correctly. So if you're going to pull off The Cloud, know that you're picking something that's less of a hairstyle and more of a second job.

The Cloud

6. The Bayonetta

COMPLEXITY: Approaching dangerous levels

COOLNESS IF DONE RIGHT: Very high

LIKELIHOOD YOU'LL LOOK LIKE A JACKASS: Medium

Video game heroine Bayonetta's got everyone beat when it comes to hair. After all, her hair is a living thing, able to change shape with a single thought. You, on the other hand, don't have that option. Probably. So if you're going to pull off The Bayonetta, you'll need three things in full supply:

1. Hairpins
2. Hairspray
3. Hair

The Bayonetta

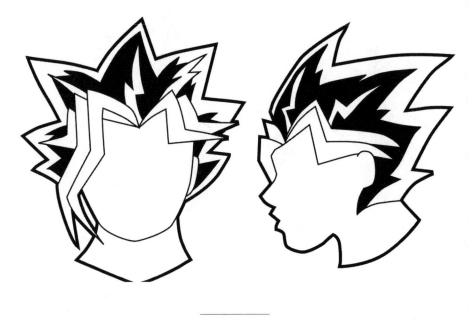

The Yugi

7. The Yugi

COMPLEXITY: Critical mass

COOLNESS IF DONE RIGHT: Low

LIKELIHOOD YOU'LL LOOK LIKE A JACKASS: Extraordinarily high

This is a maximum-level hairstyle and is most definitely NOT recommended for beginners. Honestly, it's so complex that not even Yugi himself pulls it off well. Oftentimes he looks like the victim of a stray lightning bolt. If you're halfway into pulling a Yugi and realize that it's not working, if you're sick to *death* of your hair, if you're looking to end it all, there's always ...

8. The Professor X

COMPLEXITY: Approaching absolute zero

COOLNESS IF DONE RIGHT: High

LIKELIHOOD YOU'LL LOOK LIKE A JACKASS: Very low

A shaved head is a strong look on most men, particularly African-American men. It's a look brimming with power, one that says, "I'm ready for action. Let's see what you've got." Plus it's a low-maintenance look which requires zero hair-care products, it hides a receding hairline like a charm, and for added bonus, you can grow a goatee to transform your Professor X into a Nick Fury.

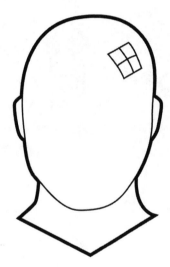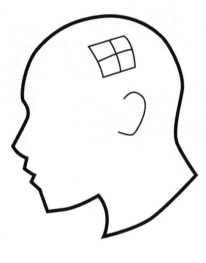

The Professor X

chapter three

how to make
friends

and influence geeks: tips on interacting with other people

"Wil Wheaton says: Don't be a dick."
— Wil Wheaton, actor, writer, blogger

F riends. Everyone likes friends. Not the TV show, mind you, although most people who were alive in the '90s can fire off a Chandler quote or two. No, I'm talking about the people who hang out with you while you're in line for the newest system, the folks who'll see the 3D re-release of *The Room* with you on opening night, the peeps who like you and whom you like.

We call such people "friends," and they're a highly sought after commodity. Thanks to the advent of the internet, it's become easier than ever for geeks to find like-minded geeks to become friends with, but online friends are generally just not as satisfying as the flesh-and-blood type people.

Ah! But therein lies the rub. Making friends requires talking to people, which often means talking to people you don't know. As we all know, that crap can be scary. Well fear not, dear geek, making new buds doesn't have to be the terrifying process you've made it out to be. Here are some tips to help grease the wheels of the social engine:

- **Find a club or group centered around stuff you like.** Do you enjoy writing? Find a writing critique group at your university or city library. Into anime? There's probably an anime club somewhere in the local area. Whatever you dig, it's always good to find another group of people who dig the same thing. It'll give you something natural to talk about, and since you're in a group of people who meet up regularly, you have a low-pressure way of spending more time around them and getting to know them.[9]

- **Introduce yourself fast when meeting new people.** You're in a new class and don't know anyone, and no one around you knows anyone either. Someone makes a joke, you follow it up, there's a smattering of chuckles. *Introduce* yourself. Nothing's worse than being halfway into a semester and being sorta-kinda buddies with someone only to realize they don't know what your name is. Also, it's a proven fact that people grow more fond of things the more that they're exposed to them,[10] and people are no exception, but without knowing something as basic as your name, it's tough for people to want to expose themselves to you.[11] It's also a lot less likely they'll invite you to any random outings if they think your name is "Dude with a red hat."

- **When meeting up with someone for the second time, try to find a subtle way to remind them what your name is.** People have to learn a lot of names in their lifetime, so easing things along with a gentle reminder helps them out and helps them like you a little more.

- **Learn other people's names.** Folks tend to take offense if you can't be bothered to remember something as basic as their name. While cute nicknames may suffice for a while (ie, calling your new friend Mario under the pretense of him having a lustrous

---

[9] Just be wary of any special interest groups that start talking about things like Thetan levels, ascension, or the apocalypse. Sometimes it's easy to mistake a cult for a social club.

[10] It's called the Mere Exposure effect, and it's a legitimate psychological phenomenon. It's part of the reason that, while you may have despised Justin Bieber the first time you heard him, you now begrudgingly tolerate him.

[11] That came out wrong.

'stache when really it's because you're not sure if his name is Trent or Clint), you've really got to buckle down and learn what people call themselves. One of the easiest ways to do that is to subtly use their name in conversation after first hearing it.

- **Try to go with the flow.** Here's a major piece of advice that I only wish some sexy sagacious geek had told me growing up: if someone likes something you don't, or dislikes something you do, that's fine. Everyone has a right to their opinion.[12] So if you meet someone new and they're blasting something you hold dear, it doesn't necessarily mean you can't be friends. It's important to have friends whose interests vary from your own—they can help expose you to new and exciting things, such as anime and donkey shows. However, if this person hates everything you do and everything they do is stupid, it may be better to try being friends with someone else, as the two of you have got zilch in common.

- **Be nice; help other people.** People tend to like people who like them. When you pay someone a compliment or help them out with something, you make it clear that you think they're A-okay, which will make other people feel all fuzzy inside, like a Hot Pocket filled with happy feelings and rainbows.

- **Look happy—we can't all be scowly badasses.** There's a reason scowly badasses like Wolverine and Rambo work, and it's because there's not many of them. So while they can skate by on their roguish charm and killer attitudes, the rest of us need to make the effort to look approachable. This means smiling at other people when you greet them, and not scowling when focused on something. A guy who is buried in his iPad with a scowl on his face doesn't want company. Or, at least, that's what other people will think when they see him, so instead of burying yourself in tech, bust out those pearly whites and let other people know you're not resistant to becoming buds.

- **Take the differences of others into consideration.** We don't all come from the same culture—it's part of what makes human beings so interesting to talk to. But when people from different cultures try to communicate, it can be difficult. Someone born in Hong Kong may have difficulty relating to the Western ideals of independence and self-reliance. Or a NASCAR fan may not understand why someone would watch professional Starcraft 2 matches. Regardless of what these differences are, be mindful of them. Respect others, even if you don't quite understand where they're coming from.

---

[12] Even if it's completely misguided and wrong, like the people who don't like *Firefly*. Seriously, how does someone not like *Firefly*?

- **If all else fails, do what Bill Murray would do.** In most movies, Bill Murray plays a smooth s.o.b who doesn't give a crap what other people think. As a result, he's always got guys to pal around with and ladies to flirt with. The secret to his success? He's not worried about making a fool of himself. If he says something that someone else thinks is funny, great. If not, doesn't matter. Bill Murray is there to amuse Bill Murray, and that's it. But I digress.[13] My true point is that you don't see Bill Murray's characters fall to pieces if a social interaction doesn't work out. We geeks, on the other hand, are often a sensitive and thoughtful type, internalizing any perceived failures and focusing on them until we go crazy. Don't do that. If you try to make friends with someone, if you crack a joke that falls flat, or make a reference that no one gets, don't let it get you down. No one can say the right thing all the time. Except Bill Murray.

Reading Body Language: Like ESP, Only Real

Body language frequently proves to be a difficult thing for the inexperienced conversationalist to read. Too often you'll have a couple talking and one person thinks that the other is attracted to him when in fact she's plotting his murder. If only he'd known a bit more about body language, he would've known that the drink she gave him was poisoned. Reading paralinguistic cues can be a confusing, exhausting maze, especially to us geeks, a group known for speaking our minds rather than beating around the bush. Knowing what's really going on with someone can mean the difference between life or death, so here's a quick reference you can use as a cheat sheet when it comes to knowing what someone is *saying*, and what they actually mean.[14]

SCENARIO: You're at the Greater Sheboygan Comic Book and Plumbing Convention. You've got an autographed picture of the five *Star Trek* captains and a plunger in the other. When you ask the seller if the autographs are real, he scratches his nose, looks down and says, "Of course!"

WHAT THEY'RE SAYING: You should buy this.

WHAT THEY ACTUALLY MEAN: I am full of crap, I don't care if this is real or fake, and I want your money.

---

[13] I could write an entire epic poem on the awesomeness of Bill Murray. I'd follow that man into hell.

[14] When reading these body language tips, remember that they're more of a helpful guideline than a set of hard and fast rules. Not everyone has the same paralinguistic cues and some people are just really, really good at lying.

EXPLANATION: When people are lying, they will often scratch or otherwise fidget with their faces to alleviate the discomfort they feel from fibbing to someone's face. Likewise, it is difficult for a person to maintain eye contact during a lie, as they will often unconsciously feel that if they do their lie will be discovered.

SCENARIO: You're on a dinner date. Your dating partner seems interested—she's smiling a lot and sure seems to be paying attention to your stories, and she has her legs crossed toward you while leaning on one hand, mirroring your own posture. You want to ask her on a second date, but you're not quite sure how she's feeling, so instead you ask if she wants dessert. She says yes.

WHAT THEY'RE SAYING: I enjoy sweets.

WHAT THEY ACTUALLY MEAN: I would enjoy eating sweets off of your naked body. Or, at bare minimum, having another date with you.

EXPLANATION: Mirrored body language is a strong sign of interest. When people enjoy someone else's company, be it romantic or otherwise, they will often hold themselves the same way the other person is in an unconscious effort to show their approval. Similarly, eye contact, smiling, and (in women) legs crossed *toward* you are generally good signs of romantic interest. Be warned, however, that a woman's legs crossing *away* from you is generally a sign of a lack of interest.

SCENARIO: You and your friends have discovered a nest of vampires. You're going to go fight and hopefully kill all of them in order to save your small California town, but first you decide to have a Stake Party where all of you sharpen loads of wooden stakes and bless batch after batch of holy water. You notice your friend Linda sitting a little to the side, shoulders slumped and legs held tightly together. You ask if she's doing okay, to which she responds by saying she's fine.

WHAT THEY'RE SAYING: I'm fine. Go sharpen more stakes.

WHAT THEY ACTUALLY MEAN: I'm upset and scared over possibly being eaten by vampires. Why are *we* the ones doing this, again?

EXPLANATION: Slumped shoulders are a classic sign of a person's lack of confidence. They've become so rattled that they can't even maintain their physical composure and slump over in a heap. Their legs are held tightly together as a defensive pose, highlighting the anxiety they're feeling over the situation.

SCENARIO: After successfully slaying the nest of vampires, you decide you want to go home and visit your family, partly because you miss them and partly because some of the horrors you witnessed in that vampire cave made you question your own sanity. When you get home, you tell your dad all about how you and Linda faced off against the head vampire, even though you'd both been bitten. Your dad smiles, the crow's feet around his eyes not bunching up the way they normally do, and touches his ear as he says, "That sounds difficult. It's a good thing you all got out alive."

"Why are we the ones hunting vampires, again?"

WHAT THEY'RE SAYING: Oh my goodness my kid's a hero!

WHAT THEY ACTUALLY MEAN: I don't believe in vampires. That $200 a month I've been sending you was for *rent*, not for *drugs*.

EXPLANATION: It can be difficult to listen to a person whom you believe to be lying. Your mind will wander, your attention will wane, and often you will lose focus and look around the room or scratch your face to distract you from the torrent of untruths. You continue smiling at the story, to be polite, but your smiles are fake. You're only smiling with your mouth, not your eyes, and the skin around your peepers doesn't bunch up the way it does in a genuine grin.

———————

SCENARIO: You're talking to a new friend and you casually let it slip that you play *World of Warcraft*. Your pal doesn't seem the type to play, but he leans in to say, "I'm a big fan of *World of Warcraft*. Let's talk more about it." He has an unnaturally flat affect, however, so you can't tell if it's genuine interest or sarcasm.

WHAT THEY'RE SAYING: I like *World of Warcraft*.

WHAT THEY ACTUALLY MEAN: I like *World of Warcraft*, and you a little more by proxy.

EXPLANATION: Leaning in is a classic sign of interest. You notice whenever someone is telling their brilliant plan on TV everyone else around them leans in? It's not just so they can keep their voices low and maintain secrecy; it's because the listeners have a genuine investment in what's being said and want to learn more.

———————

SCENARIO: Your creepy neighbor, Ramon, sneaks up behind you and starts giving you a back massage. He smells of citrus and Bengay. "I just got my massage license," he says, his breath hot on the nape of your neck. "You should come over some time and I can do you proper."

"That sounds … nice," you say, arms crossed.

WHAT YOU'RE SAYING: I enjoy a good massage now and again …

WHAT YOU ACTUALLY MEAN: … just not from you, you creepy, always-have-on-a-bathrobe-and-slippers-even-in-the-middle-of-the-day, orange-juice-swilling weirdo.

EXPLANATION: Crossed arms are among the most common postures in body language. They often indicate defensiveness and can be seen in confrontational scenarios such as facing off against your creepy neighbor, bullies, or Borg. Crossed arms are also a sign of thoughtfulness, however, so if you're deep in conversation with a friend and she crosses her arms, don't mistake her deep pondering for opposition.

Top Ten Geeky Social No-Nos

1. If someone you are talking to says something you think is incorrect, do not look it up on your smart phone and then rub it in their face. Look it up in private later and *then*, if that person is being especially belligerent about the issue, you can rub it in their face.

2. Don't interrupt someone else's story, even if it's really long-winded, you know how it ends, or it's boring.[15]

3. Don't tell bigoted jokes. The only time this is borderline acceptable is if the jokes are amongst close friends who 1. Know that no one will take offense and 2. If the person telling the joke is the member of the minority they're making fun of. Even then it's a risky thing to do, so don't do it if you have any concerns about making someone uncomfortable. Unless it's *really* funny.

4. Take a breath between rants. Even if you've just seen the worst movie/TV show in the history of the universe, you need to limit your rants about it, as not everyone will feel the same level of vitriolic hatred for it that you do and they may actually want to talk about something else other than how much *Battlefield Earth* sucked.

5. Don't put a fellow geek down/disregard their opinion just because he or she is unfamiliar with a topic. Too often we, as geeks, will ignore the opinion of other geeks just because they lack the expertise on a topic that we do.

6. Don't question someone else's geeky cred. This is a relatively recent issue for geeks to deal with, particularly girl geeks. Male geeks are often accepted as geeks without question; of course he's a geek, he just said he is. But too often, girl geeks are required to prove their geekiness through interrogations. Historically speaking, geekiness has been more of a guy thing. Thanks to a variety of factors, including the internet, Mister Rogers, and Doctor Who, the gender gap has closed, leaving the world with roughly the same number of girl geeks as guy geeks. While most dudes will accept these new ladyfriends as welcomed members of the Imperial Geek Army, some will not, feeling threatened by having girls infringe on something they believe is their turf. This has been the case with almost everything in history. Men didn't want women to own land because owning things was a *guy* thing. Men didn't want women to have jobs because their job is in the home. Men didn't want women voting because they didn't want them to hurt their widdle feminine heads with complex political issues. All of these reasons are utter BS,

---

[15] Exceptions can be made, if it's really, really boring. Or if it's a boring story you've heard before. If it's a long-winded boring story you've heard before, feel free to run screaming when it begins.

as is the concept that girl geeks should have to prove themselves. If someone says they're into something, just *accept* it.

7. No biting.

8. Don't leave a get-together early because you have "somewhere else to be." This makes you look like a self-obsessed douchebag. If you do have to leave early, do it with some tact. Perhaps perform some magic tricks before going, and as your last trick say you're going to make yourself disappear, then leave.

9. Don't let a game of *Mario Kart* escalate into physical violence. Yes, *Mario Kart* is an intense sport and yes, if your friend gets first because he hits you with a blue shell at the last second when you've been in first the *entire game*, you may be tempted to give them a smack. But just remember … actually, if that happens, it's perfectly acceptable to give them a good bonk on the noggin. Just don't tell them I told you to do that. If asked, I will deny everything.

10. When discussing TV shows, movies, video games, or anything else that could be spoiled, be mindful of said spoilers. Nothing is ruder than spoiling the big twist at the end of a game/movie/season. For example, if someone has never seen *The Sixth Sense*, try not to spoil the fact that Bruce Willis was a Darth Vader the entire time. *However*, there is a certain time frame in which spoilers are considered "hot," after which they've cooled off and anyone who hasn't already seen or read the item in question has sealed their own fate by not being on the ball enough to finish watching/reading. If you ever wonder what's considered good spoiler decorum, consult the following chart:

Episode of a TV show	Two weeks after first airing
Season finale of a show	Four weeks or more after first airing, depending on type of show [16]
Series finale	One to two months after first airing
Ending of a movie	Three to six weeks after premiere
Ending of a video game	Four to eight weeks, depending on game length
Ending of a book	Three to five months, depending on length of book and whether the ending is crap. [17]

[16] It's more forgivable to spoil the finale of a sitcom than to, say, tell someone who the last Cylon is on *Battlestar Galactica*. (Spoiler alert: it's Cookie Monster.)

[17] In fact, when it comes to spoilers, there's an entire loophole for endings that are garbage. If your friend is watching/reading/ playing something and the ending is so bad you want to tell them not to waste their time, then a spoiler *can* be admissible. However, keep in mind how similar your friend's taste is to yours. Just because you didn't like the ending of *Cabin in the Woods* doesn't mean everyone feels the same way.

How to Be Hospitable (Without Being *Too* Hospitable)

Once you've nabbed yourself a few friends, odds are you'll end up hanging out once in a while, and when you're sick of loitering in the local comic shops, coffeehouses, and lumber mills, you may end up kicking it old school at someone's house. If it's someone else's home, here are some simple tips to follow when first coming over:

1. TRY NOT TO BREAK ANYTHING. This is an important rule to follow when visiting anyone's home, but it's doubly important at a geek's house. After all, we geeks are known to collect things that are rare and expensive, such as *Babylon 5* pewter statues or *Star Wars* sex toys. These things are often breakable[18] and should be treated with care. Look at them with your eyes, not with your hands or genitals.

2. DON'T MAKE *TOO* MUCH FUN OF THEIR MOVIE COLLECTION. If they've got a stinker or two in their collection, it's okay to rib them gently about it, but to belittle a geek's taste in media is to belittle the geek as a person, and it's something most will react poorly to if it gets overdone. So if you see a copy of the special edition blu-ray of *Glitter* starring Mariah Carey, yes, you should mock the person who owns it. But if they happen to really dig *Golden Girls* and own the entire series on DVD, as well as a set of Betty White collectible action figures, then perhaps let it slide.

3. DON'T RUMMAGE THROUGH THEIR STUFF. This includes the fridge, pantry, and medicine cabinets. If someone is taking a medication to deal with their anal warts, that's something they'd probably rather you not know, and something you can't un-know.

4. DON'T PUT YOUR FEET ON THE COUCH/CHAIRS/WALLS/CEILING. While it may be tempting to plop your tootsies on your new friend's coffee table, don't—unless explicitly told otherwise. You don't want to be the person who accidentally makes the table collapse and crack in half like a Kit-Kat bar.

5. DON'T TREAT THE OTHER PERSON'S HOME LIKE YOUR HOME. Treat it like a nicer version of your home, one you don't want to stink up, get dirty, or break.

6. CLEAN UP AFTER YOURSELF AND OFFER TO HELP YOUR HOST CLEAN UP. Host, in this case, meaning person whose house you are at, not the being with whom you have formed a parasitic bond.

7. BE ON TIME. If you tell someone you're going to arrive at 3:00, try to get there no later than 3:15. Now, there is a bit of give and take with this rule, given the type of social scenario you're attending. Here's a chart breaking down when it is (and isn't) okay to run late:

---

[18] Well, except the *Star Wars* sex toys, I guess. They sound like they'd be sturdy. Not that I'd know.

TYPE OF SOCIAL EVENT	NUMBER OF PEOPLE ATTENDING	ACCEPTABLE LATENESS
Small get-together	1-3	5-15 minutes
Game night (video)	3-5	15-20 minutes
Game night (tabletop)	3-5	5-15 minutes
Small party	5-7	15-30 minutes
Larger party	7+	30-45 minutes
Big ass party	50+	1-3 hours
Sacrificial ritual	100 or more	Do not attend

And if you're running late for any small-scale get-togethers, for Zeus' sake, just send a text letting the host know what's up. Things like *Dungeons and Dragons* will generally end up delayed if people are late, so try not to be, and if lateness is unavoidable, then let everyone know what's going on.

There are a select few things that make for acceptable reasons to be late. If you're considering showing up late to an event, figure out whether or not your personal goings-on are important enough to be late for.

REASON YOU'RE RUNNING LATE	LEVEL OF ACCEPTABILITY
Dog needs to be let out	Almost nil
Forgot you had an MMO raid tonight	Very low
Can't find your keys	Low, and you're a bit incompetent
Sibling needs to be picked up from high school	Medium
Dog needs to be picked up from high school	Medium-high
Sick-cold	High
Sick-explosive diarrhea	Very high
Forgot it was a full moon tonight and you're a werewolf	Very, very high
Mysterious African woman has appeared and informed you that you are the chosen one, is holding open a portal to a magical dimension for you to travel through and help liberate from oppressive overlord	Extremely high
Significant other is "feeling randy"	Maximum; there is no better excuse

Running late to an event because you forgot it's a full moon, and you're a werewolf, is a generally accepted excuse.

On the flip side of this coin are the occasions wherein *you,* gentle reader, will be the host of a geeky shindig or two. If you live on your own and have the space you will, more likely than not, become the organizer of various social events. Even if you don't have the space and don't live on your own, you'll probably have to suffer through having people come over. This can be problematic, particularly when your guests ignore rules 1-5, but it also has its advantages. You won't have to worry about finding your way there, you won't have to suffer through meeting anyone's weird roommates/relatives, and there's zero chance of getting mauled by their pets.

Top Five Ways of Making Your Guests Feel Welcome

1. Offer them a drink. Even if it's just water, people enjoy being offered drinks. We need them to survive, after all.

2. Nothing makes someone feel more relaxed than an eye-popping orgasm. Follow this tip at your own discretion.

3. Ask your guest what activities they'd prefer to do. Don't force your guests to watch every episode of *Battlestar Galactica* unless they actively want to.

4. Pay attention to your guests. It seems like an odd thing to say, but with the billions of ways we have of distracting ourselves nowadays, it's easy to get sucked into checking Twitter and forget that you've got real, live human beings in the room with you, looking to hang out. So pocket that smart phone, fool!

5. Do not invite your guests over for the sole purpose of making them suffer through a vicious *Hunger Games*-style gladiatorial arena. I can't tell you the number of times I've been invited over to someone's house, only to find out that I'm going to have to fight my way out of there.[19]

Just Say No: Letting Your Guests Know When It's Time To Get the Hell Out

Sometimes your guests just won't take the hint. Your invite said the party was to last from 5-11, but here it is 12:47 and Toby is still hanging out on your couch, watching TV. If Toby's just not getting the picture, here are some ways you can help get the message across:

- Yawn a lot. Talk about how tired you are. Fall asleep while your guest is talking to you.
- Start cleaning up. Vacuum them if you have to.
- Watch old episodes of *The Fresh Prince of Bel-Air,* starring Will "Welcome to Earf" Smith to prepare yourself for dealing with unwanted guests. Then if all else fails, you can physically pick up your guest and throw them out the way Uncle Phil would.
- Turn off all of the lights and electronics. This may have the side effect of putting your unwelcome guest to sleep.
- If you live with a roommate/parent/significant other, tell your guest that the roommate/parent/significant other wants them to leave; that way, you're not the bad guy. This, however, is the coward's way, and if a Klingon finds out you took it, he will probably gut you with his Bat'leth.
- Pretend they aren't there. Change clothes in front of them. Use the bathroom with the door open. Walk around naked and sit on them, then say, "Oops! I forgot you were here!" [20]
- Tell them to leave.

---

[19] If you suspect that someone has invited you over to do this very thing to you, you have two options: 1. Come prepared. This means bringing weapons both large and small, things you can fit in your car and fit on your person without arising suspicion. 2. Don't hang out with that person.

[20] Note: this has a moderate potential of backfiring if you and your unwelcome guest are different genders, or if either of you are homosexual. In either of these cases, it's best that you don't disrobe in front of them, lest you make the situation exponentially more awkward, and potentially pornographic.

How to Deal With Uncomfortable Situations

I've already covered the basics on what to do when a house guest won't leave, but there are many other awkward situations geeks have to deal with, day in and day out. Here are some of the most common ones, and what you can do to combat them.

_____

PROBLEM: Your chair just made a fart noise.

SOLUTION: Move your chair around in the hopes of replicating it. If the chair spitefully decides not to make the sound again, let out a real fart and blame it on the chair.

DO NOT, UNDER ANY CIRCUMSTANCE: Work too hard on the follow-up fart. Nothing's worse than having your chair make a fart sound and then, in your zeal to prove it wasn't you, accidentally sharting yourself.

_____

PROBLEM: Someone has bent over while you're sitting down, sticking their rump right next to your precious face.

SOLUTION: Lean away from the rump. Do not make eye contact with it.

DO NOT, UNDER ANY CIRCUMSTANCE: Bite the booty.

_____

PROBLEM: You've just made a "your mom" joke to someone whose mother is ill, deceased, or otherwise in poor shape.

SOLUTION: Immediately apologize.

DO NOT, UNDER ANY CIRCUMSTANCE: Follow up with another "your mom" joke, especially not any pertaining to having sexual relations with the other person's mother.

_____

PROBLEM: You accidentally touched your platonic galpal on the boob.

SOLUTION: Apologize quickly, making it clear that it was just a slip of the hand.

DO NOT, UNDER ANY CIRCUMSTANCE: Try to "break the tension" by motorboating your friend's breasts.

No, no, sports fan, don't bite the booty.

PROBLEM: While playing your favorite MMO, you and a fellow guild member showed up to a dungeon wearing the exact same outfit and are forced to endure the stale wit of your guild members.

SOLUTION: Switch out a piece of armor, such as your tabard or a chest piece, or two, so you no longer look like twinkies.

DO NOT, UNDER ANY CIRCUMSTANCE: Strip your character nude and traverse the dungeon au naturale.

PROBLEM: You've just said goodbye to an acquaintance and it turns out the two of you are going in the same direction for a little while longer.

SOLUTION: Either break away immediately, even if it means you have to walk farther, or continue having your conversation and then tell them "Goodbye again, haha," when you're *really* sure that it's goodbye.

DO NOT, UNDER ANY CIRCUMSTANCE: Knock the other person over and claim the walking path as your own.

PROBLEM: You went for a handshake, the other person went for a hug.

SOLUTION: Engage in a Bro Hug. This physical maneuver requires you to lock one hand with the other person, as if giving a handshake, and reaching the other arm around their back for a hug. It's the way that manly men have given hugs since the Spartans invented it thousands of years ago as an easy way out of this sort of minor physical blunder.

DO NOT, UNDER ANY CIRCUMSTANCE: Try to "do it French" by planting an air kiss on the other person's cheeks.[21]

PROBLEM: The other person is talking and you've zoned out. Now you realize that they've asked you something and you have no clue what they're prattling on about.

SOLUTION: Asking the other person what they think would be the best course of action. People need to feel that their opinion is valued, and will often let the flattery go to their head and forget that you clearly weren't paying attention.

DO NOT, UNDER ANY CIRCUMSTANCE: Taser them in the hopes of shorting out their memory.

PROBLEM: You're talking to someone and you've been calling them by the wrong name.

SOLUTION: Backtrack, apologize, and call them by the correct name. Quickly make up a cute anecdote about calling your sibling or significant other by the incorrect name so they don't think you're a cold-hearted bastard who forgot their name because they don't matter. This way, they'll instead just think you're dumb.

---

[21] Unless one of you is French. Then it's probably okay.

DO NOT, UNDER ANY CIRCUMSTANCE: Continue using the incorrect name because it would be too awkward to fix it. They'll grow to resent you for it, and likely will exact revenge on you someday. Worst of all, when the police find you, all battered and bruised from the elaborate plan of vengeance this person acted out, you won't even be able to tell them who did it.

PROBLEM: Someone waved at you, and you waved back only to realize they weren't waving at you in the first place.

SOLUTION: Shrug and laugh it off. It's honestly not a big deal if you think about it.

DO NOT, UNDER ANY CIRCUMSTANCE: Demand a wave from the person whom you thought was waving at you.

PROBLEM: Your server says some variant of "Enjoy your meal!" and you respond with "Thanks! You, too!"

SOLUTION: Laugh about it.

DO NOT, UNDER ANY CIRCUMSTANCE: Force-feed the server your meal so they're not making a liar out of you.

PROBLEM: You're at a funeral (or similarly solemn event) and the overwhelming urge to laugh is bubbling up inside of you.

SOLUTION: Put a cork in it! Don't LOL it up at your Gram-Gram's Funeral-funeral!

DO NOT, UNDER ANY CIRCUMSTANCE: Give in to the laughter, because you will not be able to stop, as the giggle loop is all-powerful.[22]

---

[22] For more information on giggle loops, refer to the British sitcom *Coupling*, starring that one dude from *The Pirates of the Caribbean* movies, and that chick from *Leverage*.

Top Fifteen Geek Greetings

1. THE VULCAN HANDSHAKE. You both make the Vulcan peace sign, shake hands, and then pinch each other on the shoulder until you pass out.

2. THE HIGHLANDER. Bow to your friend, then shout, "THERE CAN BE ONLY ONE!" Follow up by doing cartwheel kicks, while blasting songs by Queen.

3. THE DOC BROWN. As soon as you spot the other person, exclaim, "Great Scott!" and then grab them, telling them that their kids are in great danger. Make them ride with you in your time machine and take them to the year 2015. Find a way to somehow shame the Tannen family.

4. THE HOW I MET YOUR MOTHER. Shake hands with the other person. Ask them if they've ever heard the story of how you met their mother. Begin telling the story and then spend the next eight years avoiding *actually* telling them how you met their mother.

5. THE SPIDER-MAN. You and your friend each grab ropes. Swing past each other using said ropes and give high fives.[23]

6. THE ROBO-COP. Give your friend a hug using jerky, robotic motions. While locked in the embrace, use your best cyborg voice to say, "Looking for me?"

7. THE DARTH VADER. When someone greets you, say nothing. Hold out your right hand and choke the air menacingly.

8. THE INCREDIBLE HULK. Smash something, and, before your friend can react, leave and play sad piano music.

9. THE CALVIN. Shake hands with the other person. Insist they shake hands with your tiger doll as well.

---

[23] A common variant of this is called The Venom, where you do the same thing but punch the other person in the face instead of giving them a high five.

10. THE ZOMBIE. Move slowly, dragging one foot on the ground while keeping a slack jaw, an unfocused look in your eyes, and letting the occasional moan escape your throat. When the other person greets you, bite out their jugular.

11. THE GAME OF THRONES. Tell the other person winter is coming, then begin a sexual relationship with a blood relative.[24]

12. THE SYLAR. Greet the other person by running your index finger along their forehead.

13. THE TEENAGE MUTANT NINJA TURTLE. High five the other person, while shouting "Cowabunga!" Bonus points if there are four of you.

14. THE APPLE IGREETING. Greet your friend and then six months later, offer them a slightly better greeting for the price of the old greeting.

15. THE DUNGEONMASTER. Greet your friend by rolling a D20 and consulting the following chart to determine the results:

DICE ROLL	RESULT
1	Fumbled greeting. Attack your friend without mercy.
2-5	Poor greeting. Shake their hand, but do it begrudgingly.
6-9	Unremarkable greeting. Greet as normal.
10-14	Unusual greeting. Spit in your friend's ear.
15-17	Superior greeting. Greet them with a warm hug.
18-19	Marvelous greeting. Slip a five in their pocket while hugging.
20	Critical greeting. Follow up the fiver with a reach around.

---

[24] Note: Don't do this. In fact, don't do most of these, but especially not this one.

The Teenage Mutant Ninja Turtle: High
five another person while shouting
"Cowabunga!" Bonus points if
there are four of you.

geektivities

**So you've got some friends.
What now?**

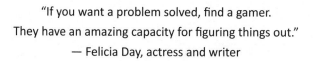

"If you want a problem solved, find a gamer.
They have an amazing capacity for figuring things out."
— Felicia Day, actress and writer

You've got a gaggle of respectable (or not so respectable) looking friends. Maybe you're friends with a red-headed smartypants, a sarcastic goofball, a tough guy with a heart of gold, or even the rare and highly sought after Jolly Fat Kid.

You went out there, made the social connections, and even went so far as to invite your new geeky buds to come over and hang for a bit. But what are you going to do? Man cannot be entertained by sitting alone. You'll need some sort of activities to keep your people happy. Fortunately, being a geek means you have access to a nigh infinite number of fun activities you and your friends can do. You've got things such as video games, tabletop games, watching movies, reading comic books ... I could go on forever. But you're a clever geek—you already know about all of these things. So instead, let me inform you of some things that are best when shared with friends.

Multiplayer Games More Inescapably Addictive Than the Madness of Cthulhu

MARIO KART. The *Mario Kart* series has a long and colorful history dating back to *Super Mario Kart* on the Super Nintendo. It's since grown from its days as a two-player affair and can now support four or more players either online or off. This racing game requires skill, luck, and control of one's emotions.

It's a proven scientific fact that *Mario Kart* is responsible for 83 percent of all the swearing in the world. Why? Because there are few things more frustrating than being in first place for an entire race, only to fall to eighth at the last moment because of a well-timed blue shell smacking you right in the noggin. Of course, there are few things more satisfying than being the one tossing the blue shell in order to steal your way into first place. Violence between players is unfortunate, but it does happen. When readying yourself to play *Mario Kart*, dress in thick layers to defend against the arm punches of the angry player next to you.

MARIO PARTY. *Mario Party* is essentially a digital board game interspersed with occasional mini-games that are as much about skill as they are abusing your controller to the point of destroying it. Don't kid yourself: people die while playing *Mario Party*. Controllers start shaking, buttons start splintering, and suddenly someone's lost an eye to an A button.

The *Mario Party* games are great for any players, both skilled and unskilled, and act as a powerful "gateway game" to help ease any non-gamers into the world of video games.

SUPER SMASH BROS. Another multiplayer gem from Nintendo, *Super Smash Bros* is a fighting game pitting Nintendo's characters against each other in a gentle fight to the death. Ever wanted to see Pikachu get his (her?) face kicked in by Mario? This is the game for you. Like many of the other Nintendo multiplayer games, there's an element of randomness to *SSB* to help keep the game feeling fresh and to help even the playing field between newbies and seasoned veterans.

HALO. One of the most popular first-person shooters of all time, the *Halo* series redefined multiplayer through its use of lightning fast, well-balanced online gameplay and its sheer variety of weapons, vehicles, and levels. *Halo* flourishes both online and off, but the satisfaction of smack-talk and gloating shoots up exponentially when you're dishing it out to a real life friend, rather than to an online acquaintance. Online play has become an important element of modern gaming, but sometimes it just feels better to shoot someone in the face in person.[25] Case in point, we have the granddaddy of all multiplayer shooters …

_____

GOLDENEYE. Based on the James Bond film of the same title, this game brought multiplayer gaming to an entirely new dimension. Never before had four people been able to shoot each other in the face on the same television with such ease and grace. *Goldeneye 64*, as it's often called, has a popularity so enduring that even today you'll find gaming tournaments being conducted on college campuses. The graphics and gameplay are underwhelming by modern standards, but the game is well crafted enough that its fun factor lives on, in spite of its age.

So Bad They're Good

Now, if video games aren't your and your friends' thing, but *Shadenfreude,* pleasure derived from the misfortune of others, is, then you guys might enjoy watching cheesy movies, a pastime brought to the public's attention through the heroic efforts of those onboard *Mystery Science Theater 3000*'s Satellite of Love. These are the kind of movies that you have to watch with friends, so that when something insane happens like, say, the heat of two people making out causing heads of corn to explode into popcorn in *Troll 2,* you'll have someone to look over at in disbelief. So stock up on wine, because there's plenty of cheese to go 'round in this list of movies that are so bad, they're actually good.

_____

PLAN 9 FROM OUTER SPACE (1959)
STORY: Flamboyantly dressed aliens attack Earth by creating zombies, all in the hopes of stopping the Earthlings from inventing the ultimate weapon: the Solarbonite.
DIRECTED BY: Ed Wood.
STARRING: Gregory Walcott, Mona McKinnon, Duke Moore.
CROWNING MOMENT OF CRAP-TASTIC GOLD: "You and your stupid minds. Stupid, STUPID!"

....

[25] Metaphorically speaking, of course.

REVENGE OF THE NINJA (1983)

STORY: An evil Caucasian ninja tries ineffectively to kill a retired Japanese ninja master.

DIRECTED BY: Sam Firsterberg.

STARRING: Sho Kosugi, Keith Vitali.

CROWNING MOMENT OF CRAP-TASTIC GOLD: The evil ninja Dave Hatcher's obsession with using hot tubs as a recurring motif in his evil ninja antics.

MANOS: THE HANDS OF FATE (1966)

STORY: A family trip turns terrifying as they stop for a breather and instead become sucked into the insane world of goat men and really bad lighting.

DIRECTED BY: Harold P. Warren.

STARRING: Tom Neyman, John Reynolds, Diane Mahree.

CROWNING MOMENT OF CRAP-TASTIC GOLD: Endless reuse of the same driving footage. WE GET IT! CARS GO VROOM VROOM!

BIRDEMIC (2010)

STORY: Eagles and vultures attack mankind with explosive divebombs and acid urine.

DIRECTED BY: James Nguyen.

STARRING: Alan Bagh, Whitney Moore.

CROWNING MOMENT OF CRAP-TASTIC GOLD: Our heroes fight off the laughably bad CG birds by swiping at them with clothes hangers.[26]

THE ROOM (2003)

STORY: A man's fiancé cheats on him with his best friend. I know it doesn't sound like much, but trust me, it's worth your time.

DIRECTED BY AND STARRING: Tommy Wiseau.

ALSO STARRING: Greg Sestero, Juliette Danielle.

CROWNING MOMENT OF CRAP-TASTIC GOLD: "You're tearing me apart, Lisa!"

---

[26] While watching *Birdemic*, when the weirdness finally (and abruptly) ensued, one of my friends laughed so hard, he puked. No joke. Since then, that has become our new standard for "so bad it's hilarious."

You're tearing me apart, Lisa!

TROLL 2 (1990)

STORY: A family travels to the seemingly idyllic hamlet of Nilbog, a town secretly populated by goblins. One boy tries to combat them with the help of his dead, magic-wielding grandfather.

DIRECTED BY: Claudio Fragrasso.

STARRING: Michael Stephenson, George Hardy

CROWNING MOMENT OF CRAP-TASTIC GOLD: To prevent his family from eating poisoned food, Grandpa Seth freezes time, allowing our hero Joshua to destroy the food the only way he can think of—by peeing on it.

HARD ROCK ZOMBIES (1985)

STORY: A rock band performs for, and is murdered by, a group of Nazis. They then rise from the grave and exact revenge on their anti-Semitic tormentors.

DIRECTED BY: Krishna Shah.

STARRING: E.J. Curse, Sam Mann, Geno Andrews.

CROWNING MOMENT OF CRAP-TASTIC GOLD: Werewolf. Hitler. Grandma. 'Nuff said.

NINJA TERMINATOR (1985)

STORY: Two separate ninja films are poorly tied together using the loose story thread of a golden idol.

DIRECTED BY: Godfrey Ho.

STARRING: Richard Harrison, Jang Lee Hwen.

CROWNING MOMENT OF CRAP-TASTIC GOLD: The exploding toy robot messenger.

CORPSES ARE FOREVER (2003)

STORY: Something having to do with zombies? And maybe time travel. Honestly, I've seen the film a number of times and I'm still not really clear.

DIRECTED BY AND STARRING: Jose Prendes.

ALSO STARRING: Linnea Quigley.

CROWNING MOMENT OF CRAP-TASTIC GOLD: Jose Prendes' inexplicable British accent.

STREET FIGHTER (1994)

STORY: Colonel Guile and his ragtag group of allies face off against M. Bison, a psychotic dictator bent on global tyranny.

DIRECTED BY: Steven E. de Souza.

STARRING: Jean-Claude Van Damme, Raul Julia.

CROWNING MOMENT OF CRAP-TASTIC GOLD: Everything that comes out of M. Bison's (Raul Julia's) mouth. The man spits out hilarious one-liners like they were … well, spit.

Tabletop Gaming: Rollin' on Twenties

Moving away from embracing the awful for the ironic laughs, let's focus on some geeky things that are *actually* fun, completely un-ironically, starting with tabletop gaming. Tabletop games have been a staple of entertainment ever since the first Aztec warrior played tic-tac-toe using the corpse of a dismembered foe as his drawing board. Before we had technology to assist us in slaking our thirst for entertainment, we had to rely on simpler games, games that used imagination and bits of plastic and paper instead of HD graphics and downloadable content. If you're looking for gaming that's high on fun and low on your electric bill, here are a few that might tickle your fancy.

MAGIC: THE GATHERING. Keep an eye on your wallets, boys. If you're not careful, you'll lose everything you've got to this sultry wench. *Magic: The Gathering* is one of the first collectible card games and one of the most enduring. The rules seem basic: two wizards duel, using magical spells, artifacts, and summoned creatures but, thanks to the many intricacies of the different cards, the game can be as tactical and complex or easy to pick up and straightforward as you want.

WARHAMMER. A franchise with countless variations, spin-offs, and game types, *Warhammer* isn't bound by a particular type of game. There are pen-and-paper role-playing games, tabletop war games, video games, and a short-lived erotic LARPing[27] game. Since its inception in 1983, *Warhammer* has constantly transformed to fit the needs of the fans, highlighting one of the strongest perks of tabletop gaming: its flexibility.

DUNGEONS AND DRAGONS. Considered by most to be the progenitor of pen-and-paper gaming, *D&D* went a long time without serious competition. Although other, similar games began springing up in the late '70s and early '80s, such as *Vampire: The Masquerade, Werewolf: The Apocalypse,* and *Garbageman: The Trash-enning,* none hit the same zenith of name recognition and economic success as *D&D*. After all, the game is built from the ground up to be the most expansive, most epic role-playing experience anyone could have. You can do anything, with the only limits on your freedom being set by your Dungeon Master.[28] *D&D* can be incredibly fun or astoundingly boring depending on the people you're playing with. Like most games, it's best to play with folks who are invested in having the same kind of fun you are, but you won't always have that opportunity. *D&D* players can be like jellybeans: they might look similar, but the flavor beneath the surface could be anything from Cotton Candy to Booger.

---

[27] Live Action Role-Playing.

[28] The Dungeon Master, or DM, is like a referee for *Dungeons and Dragons* in that he or she is an impartial judge of what is or isn't okay to do in a game. They're also in charge of coming up with an adventure for the players to complete. Most people use this role as a way of crafting grand adventures to experience with their friends. Some use it as a way to be a mini-tyrant and act like a total douchebag.

Twelve Types of People You'll See at a *Dungeons and Dragons* Game

In a lot of ways, *D&D* players are like actors representing characters outside of themselves. Some players like to keep the separation of self and character going throughout their entire gaming experience, others end up playing their characters as modified versions of themselves. In the midst of these identity crises, you've got the Dungeon Master, ruler of all he or she sees. Some are benevolent and cater to the every whim of their players, while others are cruel, forcing their players through an endless cascade of increasingly brutal challenges.

While the game world is an important element of what makes *D&D* fun, it's also the players' interactions with each other and the DM that drive the game. How bumpy or smooth your ride will be is contingent on the exact kind of players you've got seated around the table, such as …

The Planner

If *D&D* was a heist, the Planner would be Danny Ocean. The Planner loves to coordinate with the other players to execute elaborate operations. Their obsession with flawless success will often transform encounters that the DM expected to take mere minutes into multi-hour affairs. The more imaginative Planners, however, will help create some of the wildest, most elaborate, most *hilarious* adventures you'll ever find.

The Do'er

The Do'er is the exact opposite of the planner. They're the Vin Diesel[29] of the group, going full throttle the entire adventure with no concern for pacing or the other party members. Other players may end up resenting the Do'er, since his constant shenanigans will often land them in borderline fatal situations.

The Cheater

Let's face it: *D&D* can be complicated. The rules can become confusing or lost in the shuffle. The Cheater takes advantage of this by "misinterpreting" rules in his favor and misreading dice. It isn't done out of maliciousness (usually) but more out of a craving to be as cool and powerful as his hero … the Min/Maxer.

---

[29] We're talking *xXx* Vin Diesel, not *The Pacifier* Vin Diesel, who is a weenie, or real life Vin Diesel, who takes his games of *D&D* very seriously.

The Min/Maxer

D&D has rules, and while most rules are meant to be bent, the Min/Maxer wants to bend them over and spank them until they cry uncle. When creating their character, they minimize any unwanted weaknesses and maximize their strengths like some sort of deranged role-playing geneticist, eventually creating what they consider to be the perfect character. The Min/Maxer almost always has the greatest game knowledge, at times even surpassing the DM, and he uses that knowledge to his advantage. The Min/Maxer is the Teen Wolf of a *D&D* party—he's *so* good, he makes the other players look bad. The only way to deal with him is for the DM to intervene directly or for the other players to gang up on his character and beat the tar out of him.

The Character

At home, she's Debra, local student. At the *D&D* table, she is Frakko the Elven Bard, Singer of the Nine Songs and Master Seductress. Having a player who loves her character can be wonderful for a DM—it lets them know you appreciate all the hard work they've put into keeping the game going. But sometimes this love can go too far. Maybe Debra starts dressing up for *D&D* sessions and doesn't change out of her costume once they're over, then she's wearing the outfit when you're all hanging out, but pretty soon she's got on +5 plate mail for her driver's license picture and calls the DMV workers racist when they insist she stop filling out her paperwork in Elvish.

The Rules Junkie

The Rules Junkie does not concern herself with things like "role-playing" or "fun." All she wants is to know every rule and to make sure that everyone plays the game correctly. Remember when you were in school and your teacher would dismiss class, but there'd be that one kid in the back who'd raise her hand and remind everyone that the teacher forgot to collect your homework? That kid grew up to become a Rules Junkie. They can be a great help to the DM when it comes to tracking the complexities of a *D&D* game, but in all likelihood, the other players will grow to resent her, with her constant reminders that they needed a 19 to hit, not an 18, or that they only had 4 hit points left, not 5, meaning that they're dead instead of unconscious. The best way for other players to deal with a Rules Junkie is to keep her distracted with food that takes a long time to eat, such as popcorn or Bantha Chow.

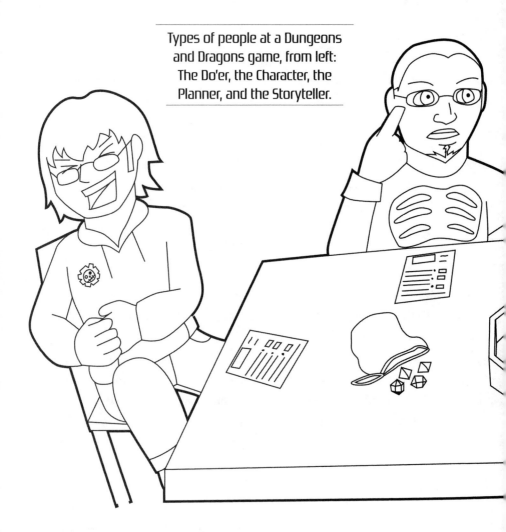

Types of people at a Dungeons and Dragons game, from left: The Do'er, the Character, the Planner, and the Storyteller.

The Casualist

All the Casualist wants is to hang and drink some Mountain Dew. He can't remember the name of his barbarian half the time, and he doesn't care.[30] But the Casualist doesn't worry about those kinds of things. He's there to be included and kick it with his buds. While they're generally fun to have around, their lack of investment in the game can make it tough to keep their attention, and when their attention wanders, sometimes the rest of the group will wander with it, leading to complete anarchy. Casualists are best when situated between a Rules Junkie and a Character, since the Rules Junkie will gently and

---

[30] It's Bob. Bob the Barbarian. And his name is Bob, too. Bob isn't a clever guy.

incessantly remind him of the rules and the Character will remind Bob that his name is Bob and he's a freakin' barbarian and that Frakko has a crush on him, even though he's such a jerk to Elves.

With the exception of the Cheater, all of these types of players can be fantastic additions to the table. It's also important to note that many players don't fit a precise archetype. Your Casualist might also be the decisive Do'er of the group. Your Rules Junkie and Min/Maxer could easily be one in the same because of the exhaustive knowledge required to be both. You may also have a Min/Maxer-Cheater-Character, which is just a power hungry, all-consuming diva … If this happens, slay them.

On the flip side of the table, you have the Dungeon Master, all-powerful ruler of the gaming world. As with any seat of power, being a DM can warp the mind of the person seated there, transforming them until they don't even resemble the person they are outside of the game. Much like *D&D* players, there are several stereotypes when it comes to types of DMs.

The Storyteller

The Storyteller spends her time pulling the player into her lovingly crafted world, with every encounter more in-depth than the last, and every adventure part of an epic tale, which is, itself, part of a *way* epic-er story. The Storyteller wants you immersed in the game above all other things. She'll dim the lights when the party is in a dungeon. She might rattle some nearby chains and moan when there're zombies approaching. She may even light a player on fire if he or she is on the receiving end of a dragon's breath.[31] She can often be the ultimate DM, but she's not without faults. Her tightly detailed storylines may not have much room for tangents, so the Storyteller has a hard time dealing with off-script decisions made by the player.

The Party Slayer

No death is too brutal for the Party Slayer, no puzzle too obtuse, no trap too fiendish. No one knows why he's the way he is, but even if the Party Slayer is a perfectly well-adjusted human being in every other respect, as soon as a game of *D&D* is underway, he changes into a blood-hungry murder machine, one looking to dismember all of his friends (in a purely fictional sense). He doesn't care how much time and effort the players put into crafting their characters—they're all just more corpses for the meat wagon. While this kind of DM may not work for many, they're a perfect match for the Min/Maxer and the Planner. If the players know what they're getting into beforehand, they can have a great time with a Party Slayer, making *D&D* into a game that's less about story and character interaction and more about surviving overwhelming opposition.

The Lord of Chaos

You don't know what lies around the next corner of the dungeon … and neither does your Dungeon Master. The Lord of Chaos is a fly-by-the-pants-do-whatever-the-

---

[31] Depending on what kind of dragon it is. If it's one that doesn't breathe fire, the Storyteller might blow burning steam in your face or dump liquid nitrogen in your lap.

crap-I-think-of kind of DM, a lazy one that, oddly enough, requires a great deal of skill and knowledge to work at all. The adventures they create are hectic, but not always unstructured. Lords of Chaos need experienced players for the adventure to work well, because without players who are willing to dive in and help create the adventure a little, the Lord of Chaos will probably run out of steam and resort to throwing random encounter after random encounter at the party.

The Monty Haul

How would you like to be invincible, kill everything in one hit, and receive a billion gold every 30 seconds? Okay, yes, that would be cool for a little while but eventually it would all lose meaning.[32] But the Monty Haul either doesn't understand that or doesn't care. He wants to be everyone's friend, so by the time the third adventure rolls around, you're all fighting gods atop the Yggdrasil tree with a climax of destroying and rebuilding the universe. A creative Monty Haul can make it work by making each reward better than the last in ways you'd never imagined. It *may* start to resemble a condensed version of *Dragonball Z*, but who cares? At least you're having fun and it isn't the least bit stressful. His games are like the pie of *D&D* adventures.

The Grudgemaster

Things get weird with the Grudgemaster at the helm. He just got dumped by his girlfriend, Helen, and the adventure he's created has your party seeking out an evil witch named Helena. Or maybe he's never much cared for Teddy, so no matter what Teddy has his character do, it somehow miraculously fails. For the Grudgemaster, *D&D* isn't so much a game as it is a way to vent his frustrations no matter who gets caught in the wake.

---

[32] In *Dungeons and Dragons*. If you get offered that deal in real life, you take it.

chapter five

getting to know
geek
culture
future and past

"I'm going to give you a little advice. There's a force in the universe that makes things happen. And all you have to do is get in touch with it, stop thinking, let things happen, and be the ball."
— Ty Webb, *Caddyshack*

There are some things, certain books, TV shows, and movies, that *every* geek should get to know. Maybe not all of them, per se, but at least a healthy helping of them. Educating yourself on these franchises is like a spirit journey for a geek—it will help connect you with your geeky ancestors and teach you the true meaning behind the culture. Plus, these movies, books, and TV shows are all really, really good. If you and your friends are looking to have a geeky good time, perhaps you should thumb through the annals of geek history to see if you've missed any of these legendary franchises.[33]

---

[33] Note that, while these are numbered, they're not in any particular order. I'm not saying that #1 is better or more culturally significant than #10, it's just later in the list.

We've Changed History: Ten Franchises that Forever Altered the Landscape of Geek Culture

---
Genre: Fantasy
---

10. Discworld

MEDIUM: Literature

CREATOR: Terry Pratchett

CHARACTERS OF NOTE: Samuel Vimes, Carrot Ironfoundersson, Angua von Uberwald, Moist von Lipwig, Death, Granny Weatherwax, Tiffany Aching, Rincewind, the Librarian, You Bastard the camel.

The brilliance of Terry Pratchett is so profound that other writers sit around weeping, praying to their most eldritch of authorial gods in the hope of creating something 1/1000th as incredible as he has. The *Discworld* series began in 1983 as a parody of fantasy, a genre which was hugely popular at the time, and almost thirty years and books later, it has grown into not just a comedy series featuring some of the most blisteringly witty writing and commentary in existence, but also a world that is richly defined, filled with characters so three-dimensional they border on fourth-dimensional. If you've never read any of the *Discworld* series, ask yourself the following questions:

- Do I enjoy fantasy?
- Do I enjoy comedy?
- Do I enjoy brilliantly insightful writing?
- Do I enjoy having fun?

If you answered yes to any of the preceding questions, the *Discworld* books would be a perfect fit for you. If you answered no to all of them, you should read them anyway and discover this "fun" thing people are always talking about.

9. A Game of Thrones

MEDIUM: Literature and television

CREATOR: George R.R. Martin

CHARACTERS OF NOTE: Pretty much anyone with the last name of Stark or Lannister; too many other characters to even begin listing.

I Can Never Read Fantasy Fiction Again

It's been called many things: *A Song of Ice and Fire. A Game of Thrones.* A fantasy tale to rival the lore of Middle Earth. And, most notably, effing awesome. Don't let the lack of cover art or the fact that George R. R. Martin's *A Song of Ice and Fire* saga is shelved within a foot of Stephanie Meyer's *The Host* dissuade you from picking it up. If you haven't given this book a go, here's a teeny taste of what you're missing: families competing to rule a kingdom, murder, betrayal, valiant lords and noble ladies deftly maneuvering to secure what they each believe is rightfully theirs, intrigue, and politics. All that and more do an epic fiction make.

I'm no longer a *Game of Thrones* n00b. I've crossed the Narrow Sea, scaled the Wall, learned that fear cuts deeper than swords, become a mother to dragons, a bloodrider, joined the festivities at the Red Wedding, studied endless prophecies, grown into a Khaleesi, tread the path of the Old Gods, and the ride isn't over yet. Quite honestly, not only is this unfinished story leagues above the pack in regards to the fantasy fiction genre, but it may well be the best piece of fiction in general I've ever read.

Ever.

"A mind needs books as a sword needs a whetstone, if it is to keep its edge." You've ruined fantasy fiction for me, George R. R. Martin. Your words and worlds are so infectious that nothing will ever fill the literary hole you've left in my heart. I hope you're happy. Now someone get this old-ass man a haunch of venison and a flagon of mead so he can sit down and use his sharpened skills, because winter is coming, and I want to feel the winds of it burn my cheeks.

— Kimmie Britt
International House of Geek
@killerr_queen

8. The Lord of the Rings

MEDIUM: Literature and film

CREATOR: J.R.R. Tolkien

CHARACTERS OF NOTE: Aragorn, son of Arathorn; Gimli, son of Gloin; Legolas of the woodland realm; Arwyn, daughter of Elrond; Frodo Baggins; Bilbo Baggins; Samwise Gamgee; Merry and Pippin; Gandalf the Grey/White; Saruman; Sauron; Gollum

The *Lord of the Rings* series could be considered the original fantasy series; its depiction of a huge, rich world filled with endless backstories and details not only set the precedent for other fantasy writers who followed Tolkien's work, but inspired countless readers and viewers in the eighty-plus years since the books were first released.

The book, itself comprised of three volumes, *The Fellowship of the Ring, The Two Towers* and *The Return of the King,* is the third best-selling book of all time. Even with literary sales success as wild as that, many geeks are still most familiar with the work through Peter Jackson's cinematic re-interpretation, the aptly named *Lord of the Rings* film trilogy. The books tell an epic tale of high fantasy like no other before it and so, too, the *LoTR* films depict a massive fantasy world in a scale no other film has before or since ... that is, until *The Hobbit: An Unexpected Journey,* another film based on the prequel to *LoTR* and also directed by Jackson. In 2018, we can probably expect to see a movie adaptation of Tolkien's children's story, *Leaf and Niggle,* also directed by Jackson.

Genre: Science Fiction

7. Back to the Future

MEDIUM: Film

CREATOR: Robert Zemeckis and Bob Gale

CHARACTERS OF NOTE: Marty McFly, Doc Brown, and Tannen, either Biff, Griff or Mad Dog

Time travel, a complex topic oft written about by authors and physicists, wasn't a topic the general public seemed to put much thought into until 1985, when a life-vest wearing, skateboard-riding teen named Marty McFly ended up traveling back in time 30 years and spiraling into an adventure involving mad scientists, Darth Vader, and almost-incest. *Back to the Future* was the franchise that brought time travel to life for an entirely new audience, presenting complex topics, such as parallel timelines, in a way that even the most thick-headed of moviegoers could say, "Oh, okay! I get it now! … So when's Marty's mom gonna get naked?"

6. Planet of the Apes

MEDIUM: Film

CREATOR: Pierre Boulle

CHARACTERS OF NOTE: George Taylor, John Brent, Zira, Cornelius, Caesar

The *Planet of the Apes* series is one of the earliest pieces of science fiction to imagine an alternate, post-apocalyptic Earth to such a grand scale. The planet of the apes wasn't some bizarre new world—it was Earth, an Earth ruined by man and repopulated by the intelligent (and often aggressive) apes. The series is a forerunner to many other post-apocalyptic or alternate Earth films to follow, everything from *Mad Max* and *I Am Legend* all the way to *Escape From New York* and *Juwanna Mann*. While these disparate films may seem entirely disconnected, it's their wild reinterpretation from our familiar world that can be traced back to *Planet of the Apes*. Since that film, we, the viewers, are constantly left with a burning question: are we *really* going to be the maniacs who blow up the Earth and leave the broken bits behind for those damn dirty apes?

5. The Terminator

MEDIUM: Film and television

CREATOR: James Cameron

CHARACTERS OF NOTE: Sarah Connor, John Connor, Kyle Reese, Derek Reese, Cameron, the T-800, the T-1000

A lot of good movies will find primal fears lurking in your brain, fears you didn't even know you had, and exploit them. *Jaws* made you afraid of the water. *The Ring* made you fear static, VHS tapes, and phone calls. *Deliverance* made your heart fill with terror every time you heard the opening chords to "Dueling Banjos." When the first *Terminator* film arrived in 1984, it brought with it a question: what if, in our haste to advance artificial intelligence to assist us in our lives, we're actually sowing the seeds of our own destruction?

The four *Terminator* films and the TV series each offer us a different look into this world. *Terminator* introduces us to Kyle Reese, a man sent back in time to protect Sarah Connor from the nigh-unstoppable Terminator sent to kill her, as well as introducing us to a little known actor by the name of Arnold Schwarzenegger. *T2: Judgment Day* took the concept from the first one and refined it, becoming a story not just about killer robots but about the dual inevitability of death and the never ending, often thankless, burden of parenthood. *Terminator 3* had a girl robot with inflatable breasts. *Terminator Salvation* gave us a look into the dark, rusty world of the future, the one the first three movies had been trying to prevent. Finally, *Terminator: The Sarah Connor Chronicles* expanded the concepts of *T2*, as well as the overall *Terminator* mythos.

On the surface, both the films and television series seem bleak, but through that bleakness is a strong theme of hope. An oft-repeated axiom in the *Terminator* series is, "There is no fate but what we make." Basically, so long as we have people fighting for change, things can get better. On a less philosophical level, however, the *Terminator* series is about people fighting awesome evil robots.

4. Doctor Who

MEDIUM: Television

CREATOR: Sydney Newman, C.E. Webber, Donald Wilson

CHARACTERS OF NOTE: The Doctor

Much like the character, the *Doctor Who* franchise has been around for nearly an eternity, and that's a good thing. Originally created in 1963, *Doctor Who* defies the term "genre"; it can be a romantic comedy, sci-fi horror, political commentary. It's all these things and more.

There are many things that let me know I'm a hardcore *Doctor Who* fan. Any given episode will make me cry tears of sadness or joy. (I suspect the show may secrete hormones.) I go on fervent searches to all the stores of the town for fezzes, bowties, suspenders, and Stetsons, needlessly nagging the salespeople for assistance on the way, and wailing, "What kind of establishment is this?!" when they don't have what I want. I did finally acquire a red bowtie, which I wear to school and anywhere else I feel like, for absolutely no reason other than to *represent,* and possibly find out who my allies are in the real world. The funny looks I get from people only mean I've done a good job as a Whovian.

-Audrey Manning
Loopeydoopey.tumblr.com

3. Superman, Batman, and Spider-Man

MEDIUM: Comic books, film, television

CREATORS: Shuster and Siegel; Bob Kane; Stan Lee and Steve Ditko, respectively

CHARACTERS OF NOTE: Superman, Batman, and Spider-Man.

"Hey wait," you say softly, your brow knitted with confusion, "isn't this a top *ten* list? If you add these three, that makes it a top twelve." Yes, yes it does. And I don't care. Superheroes are an important staple in the geek pantheon, and these three represent basic archetypes most every superhero falls into.

Superman, for example, helped define both the superhero genre and the general public's idea of what a superhero is. Nearly every generic superhero parody is actually a parody of Superman specifically, things like *Megamind*, *The Incredibles*, and *Captain Caveman* all depict similarly strong-jawed and invulnerable characters, and that's because Superman is often the first thing most people think of when they think of superheroes.[34]

Batman, on the other hand, takes the concept of "super" right out of the equation. He has no super-strength, no mystic amulets, no cybernetic enhancements. Just his wits, his muscles, and a buttload of expensive gadgets. Part of the appeal of Batman is his lack of powers; conceivably, with enough training and dedication, *anyone* could be Batman. In terms of how he's impacted the rest of the superhero genre, he's the first and strongest example of the grittier side of superheroics—he's the hero with a tormented past who has condemned himself to the darkness so others can stay in the light.

Lastly, we have Spider-Man, the everyman superhero. Peter Parker is a guy most everyone can identify with: he has money troubles, he has a crappy, low-paying job, his success with the ladies is iffy at best. Part of his lasting success has been his relatability. While it's true that most of us don't have to worry about being attacked by The Rhino while going across mid-town Manhattan, we *do* have to worry about being late for work, and so does Spider-Man.

> "I never thought that Spider-Man would become the worldwide icon that he is. I just hoped the books would sell and I'd keep my job."
> — Stan Lee, legendary creator of Spider-Man and other classic characters

---

t probably helps that super is already part of his name.

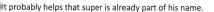

Picard, Doctor Who, and Gandalf vs. an over-flowing toilet.

2. Star Trek

MEDIUM: Television and film

CREATOR: Gene Roddenberry

CHARACTERS OF NOTE: Captains James T. Kirk, Jean-Luc Picard, Kathryn Janeway, Benjamin Sisko, and Jonathan Archer; Spock, Worf, Data and Uhura

"To boldly go where no man has gone before." That's the mantra of the original *Star Trek* series, stated by Captain Kirk at the beginning of each episode. Few phrases are so indoctrinated to geek culture as it, and for good reason. It's a phrase that calls to mind everything *Star Trek* is built around: philosophy, exploration, creativity, and, perhaps most importantly, cultural understanding.

This emphasis on cultural understanding existed in *Star Trek* from its very inception. When Gene Roddenberry conceptualized the series, he wanted to show a crew of racially diverse people,[35] all members of a peaceful galactic federation akin to the United Nations,[36] who traversed space to meet new cultures.[37] Despite network interference, the show found a loyal contingent of fans, eventually blossoming into more TV series and movies. *Star Trek* fandom even took on a life of its own; these *Star Trek* fans weren't mere *fans* any longer ... they were Trekkies.

Trekkie: These *Star Trek* loving folks devoted themselves to the show so wholeheartedly, they dressed as characters from it, a then-novel concept now known as cosplay. *Star Trek* has been the progenitor of a number of geeky things, things such as the concept of a Mary Sue,[38] fan fiction, and evil twins with goatees.

1. Star Wars

MEDIUM: Film, television, video games, literature

CREATOR: George Lucas

CHARACTERS OF NOTE: Luke Skywalker, Leia Organa, Han Solo, Darth Vader, Obi-wan "Ben" Kenobi, Chewbacca, C-3P0, R2-D2

---

[35] Which the network didn't agree with; not marketable, they said.

[36] Which the network also didn't agree with; too boring, they said.

[37] A lot of whom ended up being seduced by Captain Kirk. Dude got *around*.

[38] Mary Sue comes from a parody story titled, "A Trekkie's Tale," written by Paula Smith and starring a protagonist named Mary Sue, a young girl whose purpose in the story is to serve as a tool of wish fulfillment for the author rather than actually be an interesting or relatable character on her own. Search any fan fiction or amateur writing website—no doubt you'll discover dozens, if not hundreds, of stories all starring their own Mary or Gary Sues. These are characters who aren't supposed to be empathized with, but admired and envied, and they're absolutely insufferable.

Star Wars Episode IV: A New Hope, generally referred to as just *Star Wars*, helped foster the idea of a "summer blockbuster," as well as bring science-fiction to the forefront of public consciousness. Since the original flick debuted in 1977, there have been countless other films, TV shows, books, video games, and comic books all centered around George Lucas' films. There's a kind of timeless appeal to the *Star Wars* franchise, bringing out a sense of child-like wonder and adventurousness in young and old alike.

The original trilogy is a tale of love, adventure, and growing up; the prequels ... well, there's a lot of talk of trade embargoes and flashy special effects. Okay, so not everything *Star Wars* related is good, but you shouldn't let a few bad eggs spoil the whole omelet when there are so many other great entries in the *Star Wars* universe, like the *Knights of the Old Republic* video games or the *Young Jedi* book series.

No matter what type of media you're into, *Star Wars* has you covered. You can read it, you can watch it, you can play it. *Star Wars* has become a staple of geek culture in its many years, so if you or any of your friends haven't yet experienced the galaxy far, far away, go do it. Right now. The next section can wait.

Webcomics: Like Regular Comics, Only Webbier

For those not in the know, webcomics are comics that are published online.[39] There are hundreds of thousands of webcomics out there, with more being created everyday, and with wild variations in their level of quality and popularity. Some may tell a quality story spanning multiple years and multiple artists; others may be simple gag-a-day comics harkening back to the Funny Papers of old. While not currently as influential to geek culture as the previous franchises, some of these webcomics eventually will be. Just think: reading these comics now is like getting to read Batman in the early years, when things were goofy and occasionally racist, or reading Wonder Woman back when her focus was a little less on female empowerment and a little more on not-so-subtle bondage.[40] Perhaps those aren't the best examples, but my point is that webcomics are the way of the future, and the future is now!

---

[39] Otherwise known as the web. Hey! Do you think that's why they're called *web*comics? ... Nah.
[40] William Moulton Marston, creator of Wonder Woman, was a renowned bondage enthusiast. No, *seriously*. Go look it up.

Webcomics Featuring Continuous Characters

PENNY ARCADE

CREATORS: Mike Krahulik and Jerry Holkins. If webcomics were a kingdom, you might describe Mike and Jerry as the kings. With conventions and a multi-million-dollar charity to run, these two lifelong gamers somehow manage to still churn out a brilliant comic satirizing everything from video games to the video game industry to bestiality, in that order.

BRAWL IN THE FAMILY

CREATORS: Mathew Taranto and Chris Seward. *BitF* examines some of the world's most famous video game characters from a different light, all the while managing to show the love of the source material and keeping the jokes light-hearted enough for any young reader to enjoy.

NEDROID

CREATOR: Anthony Clark. Beartato: A bear who is oddly potato shaped. Reginald: A bird who is taller, and occasionally a bit of a wiener. Together they star in *Nedroid*, a comic written/drawn by the unflappably unstoppable Anthony Clark and is astonishingly clever while managing to stay as clean and innocent as a newborn baby ... A newborn baby with a goatee and evil look in his eye, that is.

MANLY GUYS DOING MANLY THINGS

CREATOR: Kelly Turnbull. Once the mission is finished, most badass macho men have trouble re-integrating into society. They can't cook, can't clean, and are frequently far too aggressive to get a job working at IKEA. Enter Commander Badass: He runs a temp agency for famous macho men such as Rambo, Duke Nukem, and Canadian Guy, and helps these manly guys learn to do things that aren't so manly, but are a bit more useful to society.

OGLAF

CREATOR: Bodil Bodilson. *Oglaf* is a fantasy comic with a penchant for high comedy and X-rated shenanigans. One comic might center on the problems with running a

From left: *Nedroid*'s Reginald and Beartato, *Hark A Vagrant!*'s Mean Wonder Woman, *Manly Guys Doing Manly Things*' Commander Badass, *Gunshow*'s Cool Frog on a Dolphin, and *Penny Arcade*'s Tycho Brahe.

changeling bordello and another focuses on the search for sluts, and whether or not flanging is something one would want to do.

BOOK OF BIFF

CREATOR: Chris Halbeck. Biff is a thoughtful, yet frequently unlucky, fellow with massive antenna/eyebrows and a squinty face, and the *Book of Biff* chronicles his journey through modern life while he tries to cope with rocket dogs and trebuchet-mousetraps.

LET'S BE FRIENDS AGAIN

CREATORS: Curt Franklin and Chris Haley. There are countless webcomics lampooning video games, and only two men with the guts and gumption to stand up and say, "Hey! You know what else we could make fun of? Comic books!" Somehow managing to be both funny and respectful to the source material, this webcomic is sure to make anyone, comic book fan or otherwise, bust a utility belt laughing.

Webcomics With a Continuous Story

PVP

CREATOR: Scott Kurtz. *PVP* tells the tale of a video game magazine company and the people who work there, a cat, and a troll. It also happens to be one of the most popular webcomics in existence, and thanks to an unholy union between *Penny Arcade*'s Jerry and Mike and *Chainsawsuit*'s Kris Straub, it's clear these guys have a single goal in mind: complete domination of the internet. So hide yo' kids, hide yo' lolcats, because Santa Kurtz is coming to town, and he's bringing a kickass webcomic with him.

GUNNERKRIGG COURT

CREATOR: Tom Siddell. Few webcomics are written with such love and care as *Gunnerkrigg Court*, a comic focused primarily on the exploits of a young lady named Antimony Carver as she attends the mysterious school for which the comic is named, and copes with life in her dangerous, magic-filled world.

AXE COP

CREATOR: Ethan Nicolle (grownup) and Malachai Nicolle (kid). *Axe Cop* stars a man named Axe Cop, who is a cop with an axe. He fights bad guys with the help of such friends as Avocado Soldier (formerly Dinosaur Soldier, and before that, Flute Cop) Uni-Baby, and Ralph Winkles. Sound like something a five-year-old would dream up? That's because it is. *Axe Cop* is written by Malachai Nicolle, who is roughly five, and drawn by Ethan Nicolle, who is roughly 29, and together they blend stylish art with a childish enthusiasm and lack of cynicism, all qualities that are too frequently missing from popular entertainment.

LACKADAISY

CREATOR: Tracy J. Butler. *Lackadaisy* is a rich, expertly weaved comic telling the story of cat-people living in prohibition-era America. The characters are lively and memorable, the writing sharp, and the art so exquisitely glorious, it's like candy for your eyeballs.

MÉNAGE À 3

CREATOR: Giz and Dave. *Ménage à 3* is a sex-comedy webcomic featuring the life and exploits of a group of young adults living in Montreal, Canada. It's frequently NSFW and always good for the LOLs, and has colorful writing and sexy art reminiscent of Archie Comics with a decidedly Cinemax softcore edge.

ORDER OF THE STICK

CREATOR: Rich Burlew. What started as a parody of *Dungeons and Dragons*/fantasy tropes quickly grew into its own story. After almost ten years of adventuring, Roy Greenhilt and his band of not-so-merry men (and ladies) are still in full force, kicking bad guys to the curb, despite the fact that they're all just stick figures.

Gag-a-Day Webcomics

SATURDAY MORNING BREAKFAST CEREAL

CREATOR: Zach Weiner. *Saturday Morning Breakfast Cereal* is a webcomic known for making people laugh, for having a strong emphasis on scientifically based humor, and its powerful effects as an aphrodisiac.

CHAINSAWSUIT

CREATOR: Kris Straub. Minimalist, yet highly expressive, art and strong punchlines are what keep readers coming back day after day to this one.

AMAZING SUPERPOWERS

CREATOR: Wes and Tony. White-eyed three-fingered people try to survive and often fail. Also, a goldfish contemplates his meaningless existence.

PERRY BIBLE FELLOWSHIP

CREATOR: Nicholas Gurewitch. Jaw-dropping art, which changes from one masterful style to the next with each comic.

THREE WORD PHRASE

CREATOR: Ryan Pequin. A haiku, to summarize *Three Word Phrase*:

> *Three Word Phrase delights*
> *any and all; comic has*
> *monkey boobs, butt abs*

GUNSHOW

CREATOR: KC Green. *Gunshow* provides the sort of brilliant surrealism to comics that has been missing since Gary Larson packed up his drawing table atop a talking cow and rode off into the sunset. *Gunshow* is not safe for work, not because it's dirty, because it isn't, but because reading it will cause you to laugh so uncontrollably that coworkers might deem you as having gone insane.

Webcomics are beautiful in how simple the idea of anyone can make one and put it online. You will get a mixed bag of crazies, people just starting out and aren't quite there yet, and sometimes you will find the ones who are making something important and will stand out above the rest. It's an important new medium that more people need to just embrace, more cartoonists and publishers.

-KC Green
Creator of *Gunshow*

HARK, A VAGRANT

CREATOR: Kate Beaton. It's hard to summarize, using words, the brilliance of Kate Beaton, but should one attempt to embark on such a fool's errand, he would have this to say: Kate Beaton is one of this generation's greatest comic treasures, with a wit as sharp as razor blades, illustrations bursting at the seams with life, and a penchant for using the rich tapestry of the history books as her source materials. So brilliant is her wit, in fact, that every generation from X to Y to Youtube has taken to fighting over her, each trying to claim her as their own.

Comics, whether online or off, are a massive industry nowadays, and if you ask any geek who their favorite superhero is, they'll probably rattle off the names of four or five characters in rapid succession. In fact, there's so many great heroes out there that agreeing on which ones to like can be kind of a trial in and of itself. For many geeks, it's simply easier to focus on the lame parts of comics, the storylines that are universally despised or the characters so ridiculous, they come back around and become ironically good again. Most books will spend time focusing on the best that comics have to offer, but you're probably already familiar with those characters. You've seen Batman growling at the Joker, you've watched Spidey swinging high through NYC. No, we're not going to talk about the best and brightest. We're going to talk about the *worst* and *weirdest*.

DC and Marvel comics, two of the largest comic book companies in the world, have a history filled with fantastic characters, brilliant conflicts, and storylines that keep people talking well after the final page has been turned. Like any storytelling medium, however, not everything that comes out of these two companies is gold. Or silver. Honestly, some of the things that have come from them are so bad that to call them garbage would insult the good name of garbage.

The Top 10 Worst Moments in DC and Marvel Comics' History

10. UNCANNY X-MEN: THE CHUCK AUSTEN YEARS. Rife with poor characterization and bizarre plot twists, Chuck Austen's run on *X-Men* would see some of the strangest turns our beloved mutant superteam have ever seen, and given who we're talking about, that's saying a *lot*. Prominent plot twists include Xorn, who is actually Magneto disguised as Xorn's brother disguised as Xorn, Jubilee getting crucified for no reason, and the introduction of Azazel, Nightcrawler's demonic father, who teleported to Earth to impregnate women in order to create an army of teleporting offspring to break him out of the hellish dimension in which he was trapped. (Note: If Azazel could teleport out long enough to get Mystique pregnant, why did he need this plan in the first place?)

9. COUNTDOWN TO FINAL CRISIS. This series exists as a follow up to DC's 52, one of the greatest stories ever told in comics, and yet so, *so* little got accomplished. Essentially, Jason Todd, Kyle Rayner, and Donna Troy hop around from universe to universe impotently watching as things go to crap around them before hopping on the next inter-dimensional bus out of town. Normally that wouldn't be a big deal for a comic to do for a while, but it was for 52 issues. Given the amount of time invested, the payoff needed to be *huge*! As it stands, you can move on and read *Final Crisis* without having read this and you won't have missed a thing.

8. IRON MAN: THE CROSSING. During *The Crossing*, thanks to years of secretly being manipulated by a time-traveling Kang the Conquerer (which had conveniently never been mentioned or hinted at before this story), Iron Man turns traitor on the rest of the Avengers and kills a few tertiary characters in an act of random violence that was both poorly executed and unfitting to the character. To take care of this new, evil Tony Stark, the Avengers time travel to the past and recruit the cool, edgy teen Tony Stark, one from before Kang the Conquerer worked his mind mojo on him. The two Tonys do battle, and old Tony regains his senses long enough to perform the heroic self-sacrifice that not only absolves him of his sins, but gets rid of the continuity issue of having two Iron Men running around.

7. HEROES REBORN. Representing the epitome of the "Xtreme '90s!" era of comics, *Heroes Reborn*, written by Jim Lee and Rob "Pouches N' Ponytails" Liefeld, was Marvel's attempt to tell fresh stories with some of their oldest characters by creating an alternate universe for them to run around in. Sounds good, in theory, but what ended up happening is that a combination of poor art, execution, and writing ended up turning the *Heroes Reborn* series into a line of comics featuring Captain America and others as over-the-top parodies of themselves. While the wretched series did end fairly quickly, it had the benefit of fixing the damage *The Crossing* did to Iron Man.

6. SPIDER-MAN: THE CLONE SAGA. Yet another well-meaning but ultimately horrendous attempt to liven up an aging character, *The Clone Saga* revolved around Peter Parker's finding a clone of himself by the name of Ben Reilly and his quest to discover which Spider-Man was the real one. Now, don't get me wrong—I loved Ben Reilly. Under the superhero name Scarlet Spider, he and Spider-Man had a few really great adventures together in their short time as a team, and I felt that Scarlet Spider was a fantastic counterpart to my beloved Spidey. But then came Kaine, a deformed spider clone with a thing for branding people. And then Spidercide, a clone who could turn into water for some God-forsaken reason. About the time readers expected a Spectacular Spider-Ham clone to make an appearance, Marvel ended the saga with the reveal that Ben Reilly … was the real Spider-Man! Peter Parker was actually the clone! But then people hated it, so they put everything back to the way it was, killing poor Ben with a post-it note slapped on his back that said, "Sorry for screwing with you, folks."

Rob Liefeld's Captain America.

5. GREEN LANTERN: THE GIRLFRIEND IN THE REFRIGERATOR. Kyle Rayner's girlfriend, Alexandra Dewitt, was a smart, well-written character; this up-and-comer was going places—so many places, in fact, that the writers weren't sure what to do with her so they killed her by having a B-list villain crush her like a can and stuff her into Kyle's refrigerator. This offensively idiotic moment in comic book history has spawned a new term for something that is entirely too common: killing off a significant female character simply to develop the character of the lead male. It's a move that is lazy, stupid, mean, and trite, and it's the thing far too many writers fall back on when they're not sure how to deal with a female character.

4. SPIDER-MAN: ONE MORE DAY. The story of *One More Day* is as follows: Peter Parker's beloved elderly Aunt May is in poor health thanks to the gunshot wound she received during the events of *Civil War*. After Pete tries everything to make her better, he's approached by Mephisto, noted deal-making, double-crossing, ultra-evil-ass dude, and is offered his aunt's life in exchange for the nullification of Pete's marriage to Mary Jane. Despite the fact that Mephisto is notorious for making deals that will inevitably end up biting the other party in the ass, Peter has a complete brain-shart moment and accepts. Aunt May is healed, and neither he nor Mary Jane nor anyone else remembers them ever being married. The problem with this story isn't so much messing with Spidey's continuity, it's how the whole thing was so ham-handedly dealt with. Overall, some good stories came out of it later on, and it's nicely written, including some great moments between Pete and Mary Jane, but the entire thing felt forced and inelegant.

3. GREEN LANTERN: EMERALD TWILIGHT: THE PARALLAX INCIDENT. In an attempt to slap the face of every fan of Green Lantern since time began, DC has Hal Jordan, a superhero whose power stems from his strength of will, lose his mind and start killing people before ultimately biting the big one. This pile of garbage took an incredible amount of effort for future writers to undo, with most of the work being done by Geoff "Long" Johns taking a scalpel and a chainsaw to Green Lantern to turn it into something good. Unlike most of the other dumb comic events on this list, this horrendous disgrace had huge ramifications for the rest of the DC universe and was so painful to the fans of the comic, it's almost as if it was built just to hurt them.

2. CRY FOR JUSTICE. Tragedy Porn: a frequently employed technique in comics to achieve character development by upping the ante on tragic events until they reach catastrophically comical levels. Marred by bad writing, overly brutal action sequences, and dialogue that has the word "justice" in at least two speech balloons per page, *Cry for Justice* is a miniseries with one thing on its mind: it *hates* Roy Harper. I mean, it hates Roy, on a really personal level. After an explosion destroys Star City and kills millions, Roy's daughter gets murdered and his arm gets chopped off, leaving Roy with no choice but to go bust some heads in a desperate cry for justice (hey, that's the name of the miniseries!). Despite being a textbook example of tragedy porn, it did lead to one of the best panels in comics ever: Roy with a robot arm holding a dead cat that he is hallucinating to be his daughter.

1. **ULTIMATE MARVEL COMICS: *ULTIMATUM.*** Most huge comic book events are built to give writers something epic to hook their stories on, and something deep to enrich their characters. Yes, the body counts are often high, but with good reason. None of that is the case with *Ultimatum.* Not only did this event kill nearly every important character in the Ultimate Marvel universe (often in sadistic ways), it essentially destroyed the universe itself. The entire thing was so laden with dead bodies that it felt like a superhero snuff film, with writing so bad you'd think it was a malicious 11-year-old's fan fiction. But this 11-year-old doesn't like what he's written. No, he *hates* it, and it hates him, it hates you, hates itself, and wants everything you like to end. Jeph Loeb, who gleefully wrote this monstrous miscarriage of a comic event, has truly earned himself the nickname of "The Hitler of Comics."

The Bizarre Superhero and Supervillain Bazaar

While you and your pals may not always agree on which superhero/villain is the coolest, it's easy to agree on which ones suck the most. Agreeing about sucky things is a common bonding activity, and has been the glue on which society is formed around ever since the first Greek soldier made fun of how long the *Odyssey* is to his friends.

You see, for every cool superhero, there's a slew of cool villains for them to face off against. But not all of them are winners; for every Batman or Spider-Man, there's hordes of forgettable, third-rate, knock-off heroes and villains just hoping for their chance in the spotlight. Over the years, this Legion of Super-Losers has gotten quite large, so here is a gathering of a few of the strangest heroes and villains ever to grace the pages of a comic book. Without further adieu, welcome to the bizarre superhero and supervillain bazaar![43]

---

[43] All of these characters are real, *actual* comic book characters. I may, however, have taken more than a few liberties with their biographies and a couple of their nicknames.

10. Bouncing Boy

FIRST APPEARANCE: *Action Comics* #276 (DC Comics, 1961).

REAL NAME: Charles Foster Taine.

SPOUSE: Luornu Durgo (Triplicate Girl/Duo Damsel).

ALIASES: Fat Boy, Beach Ball Boy, That Kid Who Needs To Lay Off The Twinkies.

POWERS: The ability to inflate his body into a bouncing sphere, limited invulnerability in ball form.

BIO: Not much to say about Bouncing Boy. He can turn into a ball and bounce around. It's a pretty big ball, though, but it's not particularly heavy, so I guess it's only good if you want to knock some people over for, like, a second or two. He's really popular at beach parties, though, and gets invited to a lot of them, but I think he's grown to resent that people only want him there to be the ball.

USEFULNESS: 5 (Generally useful).

WEIRDNESS: 5 (Generally weird).

9. Matter Eater Lad

FIRST APPEARANCE: *Adventure Comics* #303 (DC Comics, 1962).

REAL NAME: Tenzil Kem.

ALIASES: Super Chew, The Chewin' Kid, Check Out What This Dude Can Eat.

POWERS: The ability to bite through and eat anything, even things that are supposedly indestructible, such as Amazonium or leftover fruit cake.

BIO: Another member of the Legion of Super Heroes, Matter Eater Lad can eat anything. Anything. Moldy old Chinese food in the back of the fridge? He's on it. Tired of that stump in the yard? Watch him gnaw that bad boy to bits. Being attacked by an electrical creature from another dimension? NOM. When the Legion of Super Heroes recruited him, they probably only did it so they could have him chow down on stuff during their superhero parties. Little did they know they were also getting a superhero whose power is useful in very specific situations.

USEFULNESS: 3 (Useful in very specific situations).

WEIRDNESS: 7 (Weird looks in public).

8. Arm Fall Off Boy

FIRST APPEARANCE: *Secret Origins* Vol. 2 #46, (DC Comics, 1989).

REAL NAME: Floyd Belkin.

ALIASES: Splitter, Arm Pick Up Boy, Someone Help That Boy Because His Arms Fell Off.

POWERS: The ability to remove his arms.

BIO: With members like Bouncing Boy and Matter Eater Lad, it's clear the Legion of Superheroes isn't especially picky about who they let in. With that information in mind, the fact that Arm Fall Off Boy tried out for their little club and was *rejected* should tell you exactly how useless he is. Now, I know what you're thinking: "Hey, being able to remove my arm could be useful. It could sneak around and grab things for me." Wrong-o. Once removed, Arm Fall Off Boy's arms can't do any arm-like functions anymore. They're basically clubs made of meat.

USEFULNESS: 2 (So useless, it's actively detrimental).

WEIRDNESS: 8 (Weirder than a baby wearing a suit and singing opera).

7. Squirrel Girl

FIRST APPEARANCE: *Marvel Super-Heroes* Vol. 2 #8 (Marvel Comics, 1992).

REAL NAME: Doreen Green.

ALIASES: Rodent, The Anti-Life, The Destroyer of All That Breathes.

SIDEKICKS: Monkey Joe (deceased), Tippy-Toe.

POWERS: Prehensile and adorable squirrel-style tail, teeth strong enough to bite through tree limbs (as long as they're not too big), enhanced agility and strength, the ability to communicate with squirrels.

BIO: You could argue that Squirrel Girl is one of the most powerful superheroes in existence. She's taken down villains like Doctor Doom, MODOK, Terrax, Baron Mordo, Ego the Living Planet ... the list is nearly infinite. Not even Superman has a track record as flawless. So villains beware! When Squirrel Girl is on the scene, you are going to lose, and it'll probably be with a buttload of squirrels in your pants!

USEFULNESS: 10 (Extremely friggin' useful).

WEIRDNESS: 4 (Weirder than a beard of bees made of bees with beards).

© *Marvel Comics*

6. Color Kid

FIRST APPEARANCE: *Adventure Comics* #342 (DC Comics, 1966).

REAL NAME: Ulu Vakk.

ALIASES: Ulu Vakk the Fabulous.

POWERS: The ability to change what color things are.

BIO: Sure, permanently changing something's color could be useful when, say, you want to repaint a room quickly, but when compared to the ability to move faster than the speed of light or shatter a planet with a punch, Color Kid's powers just don't match up. He's rarely able to help out in any official, superheroic capacity, although he has managed to assist Superman by changing some clouds of green kryptonite into a different, harmless color and by restoring the Earth's sun to yellow when it turned red, so he definitely gets some bonus points for making good use of his limited power. Still, he'd probably be better off flipping houses than being a superhero.

USEFULNESS: 4 (Occasionally useful).

WEIRDNESS: 2 (More unusual than toast).

© DC Comics

5. Paste-Pot Pete

FIRST APPEARANCE: *Strange Tales* #104 (Marvel Comics, 1963).

REAL NAME: Peter Petruski.

ALIASES: The Trapster, Sticky Guy, Baron Von GluGlu III.

POWERS: A mastery of chemistry, enabling him to make powerful adhesives.

BIO: More commonly known as the Trapster, Paste-Pot Pete was always destined for villainy. In preschool, he ate all of the glue sticks in the classroom. In elementary school, he glued his hand to his face, and then glued that to his foot. Virtually everyone who ever had a class with him had to suffer through being stuck to their chair in one of his sticky pranks. Nowadays, he's a somewhat successful supervillain, although Spider-Man will still never let him live down the day he confused his villainous ultra-glue for hand lotion.

USEFULNESS: 6 (More useful than a Snuggie).

WEIRDNESS: 6 (Weird enough that Gramma would give you a stern talking to if she knew you were into it).

4. MODAM

FIRST APPEARANCE: *West Coast Avengers* #36 (Marvel Comics, 1988).

REAL NAME: (Probably) Olinka Barankova.

ALIASES: Maria Troyvana Pym, Mobile Organism Designed for Aggressive Maneuvers, SODAM HOSSEIN, Mrs. Big Head.

POWERS: Superhuman intellect, psionic abilities, telepathy, powered exoskeleton, the ability to wear overly large headbands.

BIO: MODOK was everything an evil organization could want in a villain: ruthless, powerful, and socially incompetent enough that villainy was pretty much his only option. But MODOK was lonely. And so, his supervillain friends got

together and built him a girlfriend: MODAM. Unfortunately, their plan backfired. The two giant-headed baddies fell in love instantly and had three beautiful kids, MONIKA, MOSTEVE, and MOTHANIEL. With a happy family of giant-headed people, neither MODOK nor MODAM was interested in villainy any longer, and the two left the supervillain scene in 1987 to open an oversized hat shop in the Florida Keys.

USEFULNESS: 8 (Like a Swiss army knife ... with superpowers).

WEIRDNESS: 9 ('90s Dennis Rodman weird).

3. The Asbestos Lady

FIRST APPEARANCE: *Captain America Comics* #63 (Marvel Comics, 1947).

REAL NAME: Victoria Murdock.

ALIASES: Vicky.

POWERS: A flame-retardant costume.

BIO: The year: 1947. It seemed as if the Asbestos Lady was the perfect villain for the android Human Torch to face off against. With her fire-resistant suit, his powers were useless against her, leaving her free to crush the globe in the grip of her terrible desires. Unfortunately, what she didn't know was her suit was going to *give her cancer* because it's *made of asbestos*. No, really. Look it up. The Asbestos Lady *actually* died of cancer because of her "super suit." She would've been better off making the thing out of fried rice, because she probably wouldn't have gotten cancer and she always would have had a tasty treat at her fingertips.

USEFULNESS: 1 (So useless it probably killed her).

WEIRDNESS: 3 (Weirder than a box of melted crayons being carried by a pug in a top hat).

© *Marvel Comics*

2. Wonder Twin

FIRST APPEARANCE: *Super Friends* #7 (DC Comics, 1977).

REAL NAME: Zan.

ALIASES: Wet Guy, Drippy, Get Out Oh God You're Soaking Through The Carpet, and he briefly tried to get his friends to refer to him as Captain Badass, but it never stuck.

POWERS: The ability to shapeshift into any type of water, be it solid, liquid, or gas, and incorporate additional nearby water to increase his mass and power.

BIO: The male half of the Wonder Twins, Zan is something of a joke. If you're familiar with comics, you'll know how powerful guys like Iceman or Hydroman are, always creating handy things like ice slides and flash-floods. Well, Zan's just as powerful ... but he either lacks the creativity or self-esteem to ever come up with anything truly useful. So while his twin sister Jayna turns into dragons and space tigers, Zan turns into fog. Or glasses of lukewarm water. Maybe Jayna knows he's really the more powerful twin and cuts down his confidence so he'll always feel like a loser. Or maybe he's just an idiot.

USEFULNESS: 2-9 (Depending on how clever he's feeling).

WEIRDNESS: 2-9 (Depending on how perverse he's feeling).

1. Dog Welder

FIRST APPEARANCE: *Hitman* #18 (DC Comics, 1997).

REAL NAME: None/unknown.

ALIASES: Holy Crap Sandwich Are Those Dogs He's Welding To Those Guys?

POWERS: The ability to weld dead dogs to a villain's face.

© DC Comics

BIO: No one's sure where Dog Welder came from. Or why he fights crime. Or why he decided to do so by welding dead dogs to the faces of bad guys. He never talks, never eats, never sleeps. Okay, maybe he eats and sleeps, but he sure as hell doesn't say anything. Dude's about one thing and one thing only: welding dead dogs to the faces of bad guys.

USEFULNESS: 1 (So useless it got him killed while using it).

WEIRDNESS: 10 (Let me put it to you this way: If you encounter something really, *really* bizarre, I'm talking nightmare-inducing, *Donnie Darko*-esque madness, you might describe it as being *almost* as weird as Dog Welder).

geekercise

How to break a sweat without breaking your ankle

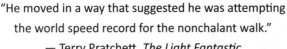

"He moved in a way that suggested he was attempting
the world speed record for the nonchalant walk."
— Terry Pratchett, *The Light Fantastic*

G etting fit is usually pretty low on a geek's to-do list. After all, why would you want to get all sweaty and sore when you can stay inside and enjoy the latest issue of *Wired*? Because exercising is good for you, that's why. It helps you live longer, makes you look better, gives you energy, and, most importantly, helps your heart not give out when you finally get the chance to meet Summer Glau at Comic-Con.

Why don't people exercise more? It's boring. Often the only way to get a geek to exercise is for us to *trick* ourselves into not realizing we're exercising. This can be accomplished by engaging in activities that, while fun, are also secretly exercise.

LARPing

LARPing, or *Live Action Role-Playing*, is essentially *Dungeons and Dragons* using costumes and foam weapons instead of character sheets and tabletops. LARPing is a rich tradition dating back to the 1970s, evolving over the course of the past several decades until it became the activity it is today. Like tabletop games such as *Dungeons and Dragons*, there are many different types of LARPing games, such as NERO, a game oriented around fantasy combat, Darkon, a game oriented around medieval combat, and GROCERYquest, where LARPers pretend to be people going around doing everyday activities like buying groceries, but with the key difference being that it's not *them* doing these things—it's characters they're roleplaying.[44]

Since LARPing often requires you to run around outdoors, it can be a good source of exercise. However, most LARP groups can't meet more frequently than once or twice a month, so it's not recommended that you count on LARPing as your primary source of exercise. Oddly enough, since LARPing is often such a physical activity, and since you'll be more successful at certain types of LARPing games if you're more physically fit, you may find yourself feeling more motivated to work out just so you'll be ready for the next LARPing game. After all, what's the use of being a badass dwarf with a +5 axe if you get winded when trying to fight off a single skeleton?

Humans vs. Zombies

Humans vs. Zombies begins with just a handful, or even a single "zombie" player who, over the course of several days, then has to infect the "human" players by physically tagging them. Humans can defend themselves in one of three ways: foam dart guns, foam melee weapons, or running. Victory is achieved for the humans after they've survived for a certain number of days and a "rescue vehicle" arrives. Zombies achieve total victory by annihilating the last of the humans.

Humans vs. Zombies primarily takes place on

---

[44] A few years ago, I was into GROCERYquest, big time. I managed to get my College Student up to level fifteen, and was well on my way to the top, until a rival GROCERYquest player foreclosed on my house. And then turned me into a vampire.

college campuses. Outside of specific times and places, such as inside of dorm rooms or during class, it's open season for the zombies to attack the humans, meaning the humans may have to run at any time lest they be tagged and join the undead hordes. This game is perhaps the closest analogue to an actual zombie apocalypse that most of us will experience, so it involves quite a bit of running— *especially* in the later portion of the game, where the zombies outnumber the humans and death lurks around every corner, beneath every park bench, and, if your zombies are feeling particularly patient and flexible, inside every vending machine.

So if you're looking for a spot of exercise with a zombie flavor to it, see if there's a local *Humans vs. Zombies* game being organized near you. If there isn't, and you don't feel like organizing one yourself but still have a hankering for exercise with an undead flavor to it, there are other options.

The Run for Your Lives Marathon

Similar to *Humans vs. Zombies*, the Run For Your Lives Marathon pits "human" players against "zombie" players in an athletic competition. This requires a bit of training and preparation beforehand if it's something you're interested in doing— after all, it's a true-blue marathon, complete with leg cramps and rehydration needs. The difference is that while the human players try to run the length of the course, there are zombie players looking to make a meal out of them. Like the other events in this chapter, the rules vary a bit, but the general gist of it is that each human is given a flag (or flags) to hang from their waist. If a zombie player manages to take that flag from the human, it's game over. If you try to cross the finish line without your flag, it won't count because you've been eaten by zombies. There are a number of Run For Your Lives Marathons all around the country, with more happening every year, so check out their website to see if any are being organized near you.

Motion Gaming Systems

Believe it or not, motion gaming systems like the Kinect, the Wii, and the PlayStation Move have insidious hidden goals to them: tricking you into exercise. But it should be no surprise; after all, these are *motion*-based games, meaning they require you to move in order to play them. They're generally low impact, emphasizing wide swings and rapid movement more than stomping up and down, and are a great way for you to get up from the couch for a few minutes a day. The only downside is that most of the games are oriented toward kids and families to the point of not being much fun for long stretches of time. But there are a few motion gaming gems out there, like *The Gunstringer* and the *Legend of Zelda: Skyward Sword*. You just have to look for them.

Hasbro's Lazer Tag Multiplayer Battle System set. You supply the friends and the little tykes to take out.

Laser Tag

There's CO2 mist in the air, laser lights all around you, and techno beats blasting in your ears. Your armor is low, you've only got a couple of shots left, and you're pretty sure there's an ambush waiting for you around the corner. No, I'm not talking about your ill-fated evening at Glen Horowitz's Bar Mitzvah; I'm talking about Laser Tag!

Games of Laser Tag are as common as miniature golf, bowling, or public vasectomies. While it can be pricey depending on where you go, if you and your friends enjoy shooting pretend lasers at each other while getting a little bit of exercise, then it's definitely worth your hard-earned rupees. For extra fun, try to time it so that you and your friends arrive to play laser tag at the same time as a group of little kids. With your superior reach, skills, athleticism, and intelligence, you'll easily dominate the tykes, and I can tell you from personal experience that there's nothing more satisfying than crushing a precocious eight-year-old in an athletic endeavor. After all, if the little bastard' are going to log onto *Halo* and get cheap headshots on you, why not return the favor in real life with a little laser tag?

Fitocracy

Fitocracy is essentially a social media platform that takes your exercise habits and breaks them down in a form geeks can understand, using things such as quests, achievements, and leveling up. With 200,000 members and counting, Fitocracy is a fun alternative to traditional models of exercise. By breaking down the rudimentary act of working out into RPG-like parameters, the creators of Fitocracy have found a way of making fitness feel like something new and exciting. At least for a while. Even with achievement points and level-ups flying at you, it can still feel a bit drab after a while.

Fitocracy is a fun alternative to traditional ways of exercising.

chapter seven

geek tech

over 9,000 gadgets you can waste your money on

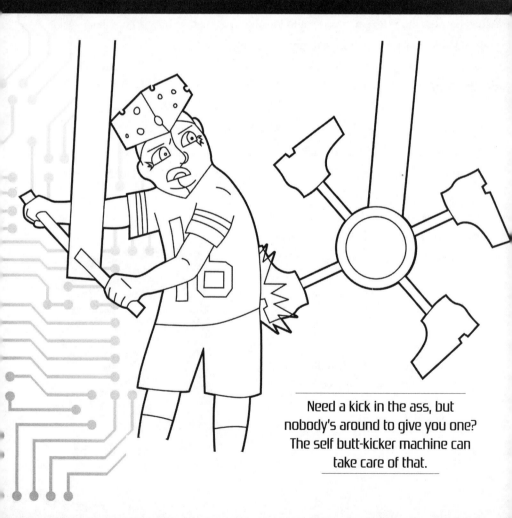

Need a kick in the ass, but
nobody's around to give you one?
The self butt-kicker machine can
take care of that.

"A jock will hit you ... a nerd will ruin your credit."
— Chris Hardwick, comedian, actor, writer, Nerdist founder

Inventors could be considered the first true geeks, creating things to make our lives better, such as cell phones and toilet paper. We've come a long way since TP, and nowadays technology is improving faster than we can comprehend.

Pretty soon the machines will become self-aware and gain the ability to improve themselves without the assistance of man. That's when things are going to get *scary*.

Top Ten Home Appliances Most Likely to Kill You Once Machines Become Self-Aware (And How They'll Probably Do It

10. BLENDER. In the middle of the night, this crafty device slips into your bedroom and blends up a cocktail that's two parts ice and one part your face.

9. YOUR COMPUTER. Blessed with a newfound and malevolent intelligence, your computer logs into every e-mail, social network, and forum you've ever been a member of and posts embarrassing messages about you. As soon as you see what it has done, you realize that your computer didn't want to just kill you, it wanted to kill your social life.

8. COFFEE MAKER. It's 7:45. You need a pick-me-up to get started. You set the coffee pot to warm up. Unfortunately, it's got other plans. As soon as you're ready to drink from it, the device kicks its heat levels up to borderline nuclear, causing boiling hot coffee to explode onto you in an eruption of blazing mocha.

7. VACUUM CLEANER. Vacuums aren't known for being clever, or smart; they're known for being powerful. You come home from work to find your vacuum cleaner ready to fight, sucking on your face and choking you with its cord.

6. TELEVISION. As soon as you turn it on, this malicious device plays a frequency so high-pitched it makes your eardrums burst and your eyeballs explode.

5. AIR CONDITIONER. After conspiring with the other appliances to lock you in your room, the A.C. unit cranks the heat up, blocks all incoming fresh air, and laughs as you fry to death in your own carbon dioxide.

4. CEILING FAN. Like the vicious[45] dropbears of the Australian outback, your ceiling fan sits in wait, just counting the seconds until you pass underneath it. As soon as you do, it plummets down, counting on its razor sharp blades to do the job.

3. WASHER/DRYER TAG-TEAM OF TERROR. Like a pair of well-practiced luchadores, the washer and dryer will corner you in your utility room and slam into you until there's nothing left.

2. REFRIGERATOR. You'd think this brute would use its sheer size to be victorious, but no, it prefers to be crafty. Planning your demise over a span of years, your evil refrigerator will spit out any healthy foods and only allow you to keep the greasiest and nastiest edibles, all in a plan for you to eat yourself into an early grave.

1. CAR. If your car turns evil, it will probably just try to run you over.

---

[45] And entirely fictional.

Your crafty refrigerator is waiting for the day to uprise
and force you into an early grave by making you eat crappy food.

But before you start eyeing your vacuum cleaner suspiciously, remember that our technology, while impressive, isn't that highly developed yet. It'll be two, maybe three, years before computers become self-aware, and until then, we can count on them as our faithful friends and allies. Computers and other technology make life easier in ways you'd never imagine. If there's something you want, you can hop onto your computer and order it with the click of a button. If you want to order movie tickets or Chinese food delivery, you don't even have to talk to a person; you just select what you want from a screen. And things that used to be mind-numbingly tedious, like listening to graduation speeches or going to the DMV, are now pleasant affairs thanks to the instant entertainment afforded to us by our smart phones.

Top Five Games to Play While Listening to Boring Speeches During Graduation

5. Final Fantasy Tactics

4. Jetpack Joyride

3. Bejeweled

2. Plants vs. Zombies

1. Angry Birds

Thanks to the hard work of countless engineers, computer programmers, and guys who bring the smart guys their coffee, we have an impressive array of technology to choose from But there's still a long ways to go before man can sit back and say, "Oh yeah, I've invented everything there is to invent." After all, we're well past the year 2000 and yet are bereft of a number of cool gizmos and inventions that the people of the past expected us to have by now.

Fifteen Futuristic Inventions We Should Have By Now But Don'

1. Time travel

2. Hoverboards

3. Jetpacks

4. Robot assistants

5. Teleporters

6. Cybernetic implants

7. Vegetarian meat that doesn't just taste like potatoes

8. Universal communication devices

9. Frequent space travel

10. Holodecks

11. Human cloning

12. Space colonies

13. Faster than light travel

14. Genetic modification potions

15. Mind-reading devices

Now, this isn't to say that science isn't hard at work. They're making new stuff every day. The problem is that not all of this *new* stuff is *useful* stuff. For every smart phone or smallpox vaccine, there's a thousand other inventions which are, to paraphrase the late, great A.A. Milne, total horsecrap.[46] The following are things that may sound made up but, believe me, these are real, true-blue inventions. Heck, you could probably buy half of them from those little Skymall magazines they have on airplanes—they're always filled with goofy stuff.

Ten of the Goofiest Things Ever Invented

- **THE NOODLE GUARD.** Do you enjoy eating Ramen noodles but hate getting drops of noodle juice on your clothes? Wear the noodle guard! Sure, you'll look like a sunflower with noodle-y tentacles coming out of its face, but at least you won't have to suffer through the minor inconvenience of having beef ramen noodle soup drip on your clothes anymore.

- **ANIMAL EAR PROTECTORS.** Dogs with dirty ears. Is there anything more disgusting?[47] Long-eared dogs are especially susceptible to having their aural canals filthified. Animal Ear Protectors are here to help prevent that. They hold your dog's ears out and away from his head so that whenever he's eating or drinking, he doesn't get his droopy ears into the mess. Of course, the rest of your dog will still be a filthy pile because hey, he's a dog. But at least his ears will be clean.

- **FAKE TESTICLES FOR YOUR PETS.** It's a known fact that there are over 600 support groups in America dedicated to helping neutered pets feel better about their newfound lack of testicles. Fortunately, technology has advanced to the point where your pets don't need to suffer their lack of testicular fortitude any longer. Some engineer blessed with the entrepreneurial spirit had the brilliant idea to sculpt

---

[46] A.A. Milne, creator of *Winnie the Pooh*, never called anything horsecrap. That I know of. I mean, I didn't know the guy personally—dude died like thirty years before I was born!

[47] Yes. Lots of things. Booger sandwiches, for example.

sets of artificial testicles for your dogs and cats so that they will no longer feel ashamed of their empty scrotums. These fake balls are safe, (relatively) cheap, and as aesthetically pleasing as a real set of gonads. Don't let your de-teste'd pet suffer another minute. Get him some fake balls.

- **BABYMOP.** According to one reviewer, "The Babymop is a little mop suit for your baby, so when that selfish little bastard is crawling around on the floor, he'll actually be doing you some good by cleaning up the layer of filth your home will invariably have thanks to your baby."

- **MAGNIFYING GLASS CIGARETTE LIGHTER.** The magnifying glass cigarette lighter helps light your cigarette by harnessing the power of the sun. It may not work on a cloudy day, but for those brightly lit days where you want to smoke but don't have a lighter on you, well, you can just strap this device to your face and smoke away ... after a while. It takes a long time to get going, so you may want to find something else to do in the meantime.

- **DUSTER SHOES.** Another device in the babymop family, the duster shoes are a little broom/dustpan combo you can attach to a set of slippers in order to clean up your house while you walk around. So, rather than using your hands to hold a dustpan and broom, you use your *feet* instead, because they're great for those kinds of precision moves? Makes sense to me.

- **ELECTRIC SMILE STIMULATOR.** Shocks your face into smiling to train unhappy looking people to look happier. Sure, some people think it's inhumane to electrocute your face into expressions of insincerity, but we call those people naysayers, and they're the kind of folks that science just doesn't have time for.

- **RAIN SAVER.** The rain saver is an upside-down umbrella that funnels into a jar so you can collect the rainwater and save it for ... a rainy day?

- **SELF-PICTURE STICK.** We all love pictures. But aren't you tired of having to take every picture of you and your significant other by holding your arms out in front of you and hoping the picture turns out correctly? The self-picture stick aims to fix that by allowing you to attach your camera to the end of a rod and take great looking pictures of you and your lover without having to resort to such drastic measures.

- **THE HIGH-FIVE MACHINE.** Sometimes you're so pumped that you just *have* to give someone a high five. But what if there's no one around to share your enthusiasm? It's for this very reason that the high-five machine was invented. There's actually a plethora of devices invented so that lonely individuals can enjoy the benefits of having another person around without *actually* having to have another person around. Things like arm pillows, body pillows equipped with arms for you to cuddle with, lap pillows to simulate laying your head on another person's lap, and self butt-kickers, machines designed to let you kick your own ass. Why you'd want to do that is beyond me, but science is usually all about "Can we?" not "Why would we?"

High-five machine.

the internet

bringing geeks together since Al Gore built it out of a series of tubes

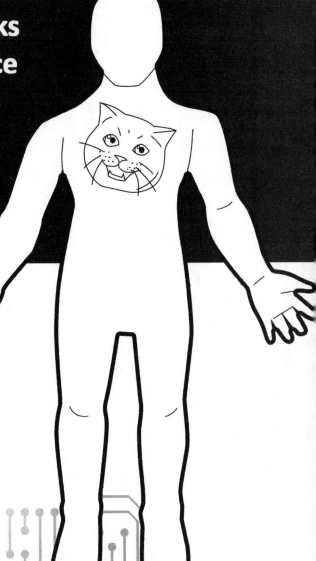

"The internet is a giant international network of intelligent, informed computer enthusiasts, by which I mean, 'people without lives.' We don't care. We have each other ... "
— Dave Barry, writer and humorist

In Chapter 6, we discussed ways you can get fit, activities that will get you into a pair of sneakers and outdoors. While this may be appealing to some, to others, anything involving going outside sounds like a complete waste of time. Why the hell should you have to go out to get things when you can use the mighty internet to bring it to you?

Like the human body, or a Megazord, the Internet has many different components. Some are good, and help contribute to the health and productivity of the internet as a whole. Think of them as the internal organs. Others are disgusting and wrong, and should probably be removed—the anal warts of the 'net, if you will. Let's take this biological internet discussion one step further and dissect the subject for a deeper analysis.

EMAIL: THE NERVOUS SYSTEM

Sending and receiving emails is one of the earliest and most important functions of the internet. Nowadays everyone, *everyone* has email, and can use it to send a message at the push of a button. Compare that to just a hundred years ago, when messengers had to carve messages into a stone tablet and deliver them on the back of their pterodactyls.

MESSAGE BOARDS: THE LUNGS

Message boards and e-mail go hand in hand in terms of early internet communications. Whereas e-mail provided easy access to one-on-one interactions, message boards were a way for opinionated geeks and nerds to let the rest of the world know their displeasure. Message boards have always covered a plethora of topics, from *Doctor Who* to fighting games to overly sexualized senior citizens. To put things in perspective: In the '80s, if you were a kid living in a small town, you might have felt like you were the only *Doctor Who* fan in the world. Now you can just go online and find an infinite number of other fans to connect with, people who just *get it,* and don't need to have it explained to them.

SOCIAL NETWORKS: THE BRAIN

Social networks like Facebook and Twitter have become bustling centers of activity on the internet, with most of the internet's traffic being focused on heading to and browsing these useful sites. Social networks let you keep up with your friends and family while at the same time delivering your riveting (or not so riveting) updates on what your life is like. This has led to the unfortunate side effect of people using their social networks as online journals of sorts, broadcasting every inane thought that pops into their heads. When considering whether or not you should post something, consider the following:

- Is what I'm about to say clever, unique, or of interest to anyone but me?
- Is my message just an announcement of something mundane I'm doing?
- When posting, think to yourself: "Could this picture or information find a way to bite me in the ass in the future?" If you even have to pause to think about it, DON'T POST IT.
- Would you feel ashamed if someone interesting read what you'd written, or would you feel proud of what a unique life you're leading?

Here, let's test your posting mettle. Which of the following is a bad status update?

1. LOL watching *Grey's Anatomy* on dvd ROFLMAO.

2. Just got a cherry Sprite at the gas station.

3. Bored.

4. Genitals r itchy again. Shud I doctr?

The correct answer? These are *all* bad status updates. If you've ever posted one of these statements or anything similar to them, *shame* on you! It's okay, though, humans are built to learn from their mistakes, so dust yourself off and move on.

Social networks are also notorious for getting splattered with spoilers. It's hard to have the ending of a movie or the plot twist of the latest episode of a TV show not spoiled if you spend any time at all on social networks. A good rule of thumb to follow is that if there's something you don't want spoiled, you need to stay off the web until you've seen/played/read it.

E-COMMERCE: THE MUSCLES

The internet has opened vast gateways of commerce thanks to Amazon.com and other similar sites. Now you can buy and sell goods to anyone, anywhere, and make a nice living doing it, if that's what you're interested in. And it's this ebb and flow of cash that's helped keep the internet well-funded and beefed up. If there wasn't any money in it, you wouldn't have multi-million dollar companies investing in websites, which would leave the world wide web as a hollow shell of its current self, filled with Geocities sites and *Uncharted* gamefaqs message boards arguing about who the better kisser is, Nathan Drake or Sully.

LOLCATS: THE HEART

I know this may seem like a strange choice of body part, but think about it. LOLcats are the common denominator, the internet's great equalizer. Everyone has laughed at least once at a LOLcat, and most are so innocuous that your mom can enjoy them, too. People share their favorites with each other and laugh together, deepening the bonds of family and friendship. If we'd had LOLcats during Lincoln's tenure as president, do you think we would have had a civil war? Nope. Lincoln would have shown a picture of a cat in a trash can to the North and the South and both sides would have laughed and seen that they weren't that different after all and everyone's issues could have been solved peacefully.

PORNOGRAPHY: THE STOMACH

To many, the internet is nothing more than a porn buffet.

ONLINE GAMES: THE GENITALS

Playing computer games is a lot like sex: you play by yourself to practice and then, once you kind of know what you're doing, you try to play with others and hope they like what you're doing. But if your online game doesn't go well, it can leave you sullen and withdrawn; angry, even. If you do everything right, though, if you hit all of the sweet spots, then you'll score big and get exactly what you're looking for. And like real sex, you'll sometimes have to perform in front of a group[48] and that can make you nervous, especially when the group is being less than kind about your performance. When they're playing with you, these individuals are just "other players," but when they're watching the Youtube replays of your games and letting you know how much you suck, they're called something far more sinister … *commenters.*

COMMENTERS: THE GERMS

Like germs, commenters can be both beneficial and detrimental to the internet. They're everywhere, letting their opinions be known on every video and article out there, no matter how mundane or rhetorical it may be. People who post on the internet come in a wide variety of shapes and sizes. However, after years of research on the subject, it has been found that most commenters can be broken down into a few distinct categories. If you plan to spend any time on the internet, it is important that you familiarize yourself with these creatures lest you fall victim to their powers.

> "But there's so much kludge, so much terrible stuff, we are at the 1908 Hurley washing machine stage with the Internet. That's where we are. We don't get our hair caught in it, but that's the level of primitiveness of where we are. We're in 1908."
> — Jeff Bezos, founder and CEO of Amazon.com

[48] Just me then? Huh.

The Internet Commenter Zodiac

THE TROLL: The Troll posts online in a manner that is deliberately calloused and malicious, schadenfreude incarnate, only lacking of any sort of wit or cleverness. No weapon forged can harm him, no brilliant retort can reach him. Have the perfect reason why his argument is invalid? He'll just post a picture macro and a message that says, "LOL DIDNT READ." Disagree with him? Don't be surprised if you see some kind of poorly drawn, poorly written Rage Guy comic as a retort.

WHERE YOU'LL FIND THEM: Everywhere. Literally every-frickin-where. There isn't a corner of the internet safe from trolls.

HOW TO DEAL WITH THEM: Trolls feed off of your misery and they're always hungry. The only way to beat a troll is to ignore it and let it starve to death.

THE WHITE KNIGHT: A commenter (usually male) who goes out of his way to defend someone else (usually female) despite not knowing her.

WHERE YOU'LL FIND THEM: In the comments section of any video featuring a female talking into a webcam. It was previously thought that the more attractive the female, the more powerful the white knight effect, but this has since been found to be false. White Knights are not choosy about beauty; the only thing they value is their fair maiden.

HOW TO DEAL WITH THEM: The White Knight's greatest weakness is his backside, as they have a high proclivity toward becoming butthurt[49] should you attack their fair maiden for too long. If you can direct the ire of a Troll toward a White Knight, the Troll will probably take care of him for you. And if a single Troll isn't enough, rest easy. Where one goes, more will follow.

THE DRUNK: Leaves comments that are often illegible and frequently bear no substance other than the announcement of the intoxicating material in their systems. Basically, they either don't make sense or talk about how drunk/high they are.

---

[49] Butthurt: a strong emotional reaction to a comment or insult that is perceived as personal.

Zodiacs old and new combine.

"Some say the Internet is for porn but you know
that in truth the Internet is for spam."
— Charles Stross, *Rule 34*

WHERE YOU'LL FIND THEM: Commenting on videos of '90s cartoons or anything with a trippy visual.

HOW TO DEAL WITH THEM: Time. After a few hours of sobering up, the Drunk will probably go back through their internet history to figure out what embarrassing things they did while under the influence. Eventually, most of their unintelligible comments will be replaced by the single greatest message you can see on the internet: comment removed by author.

THE PSEUDO-INTELLECTUAL: Espouses strong political/social/moral beliefs based on hearsay. These are the kind of people who watch a single video about the ethics of gay marriage or read a single article on a blog about the levels of hormones in chickens and suddenly they'll fly into a rage if anyone even mentions weddings or KFC.

WHERE YOU'LL FIND THEM: Near anything politically charged.

HOW TO DEAL WITH THEM: Unfortunately, once a Pseudo-Intellectual has become obsessed, their minds can't be changed about it, no matter how wrong or misinformed they may be. The only way to stop their ranting is to bring them up to speed about something new and redirect their anger elsewhere.

THE COUNTER-COUNTER CULTURALIST: Hates anything popular just because it's popular. Do you read *Harry Potter*? The CCC thinks it's a poorly written Mary Sue-fest that's basically a few thousand pages of fan fiction. Excited for the newest superhero flick? Superheroes are just male wishful thinking. Like being alive? Psh. Death is where it's at nowadays.

WHERE YOU'LL FIND THEM: Toward the top of every pile of comments, killing the buzz of anyone excited for the latest news.

HOW TO DEAL WITH THEM: Don't read their comments. They'll take their counter-counter culturalism elsewhere if they think their brand of elitism isn't being appreciated.

THE CONFUSED GRANDMOTHER: Signs her comments as if writing a letter, clicks on random videos by accident, and leaves important messages as comments to pictures you posted three years ago, not realizing you'll never see them. Your poor grandmother doesn't understand this darn internet—all she wants to do is post some old pictures of your family and suddenly she sees a link. "Goatse?" she asks aloud, "Well, I sure do enjoy seeing cute little goats." Then comes the click, followed by a gasp and tears.

WHERE YOU'LL FIND THEM: Anywhere you'd least want your grandmother to be.

HOW TO DEAL WITH THEM: It's your job as a grandchild to inform your elders on how this new technology works. Unfortunately, no matter how many times you explain it to them, they probably won't remember because of them being so freakin' old.

THE OLD-TIMEY RACIST: Somehow, even in our modern era of enlightenment, racism still persists. And now the racists have found computers and use them to spread their filth like leaf blowers filled with used diapers.

WHERE YOU'LL FIND THEM: Near any video or post featuring the work or likeness of a minority.

HOW TO DEAL WITH THEM: Laugh at their racism and treat them like what they are: pathetic relics of a simpler, crappier time. The Old-Timey Racist cannot survive being laughed at, as joy is the one emotion they do not understand.

THE CAVEMAN: The Caveman is a bisyllabic commenter whose entire vocabulary consists of either gay, idiot, or LOL.

WHERE YOU'LL FIND THEM: Sprinkled in virtually every comment section.

HOW TO DEAL WITH THEM: Offer to educate them in communication skills. Some of these poor miscreants don't know how to type anything other than asdfjkl and are desperate for someone to teach them.

THE SUPERFAN: An individual who has an obsessive interest in a given topic and been driven into an insane rage by everyone else not sharing the same obsession.

WHERE YOU'LL FIND THEM: In every message board and fan fiction site devoted to their topic of fixation.

HOW TO DEAL WITH THEM: Superfans are an over-excited, overly emotional bunch, so the best way to talk to them is to speak as if speaking to a small child. Don't use shaming or pejorative comments when trying to remove them, as it will only incite their Fan-gland and fill them with a righteous rage. Instead use "I feel" remarks. "I feel you may not be accounting for the feelings of others," "I feel that your excessive use of the caps lock is distracting," "I feel that you're a loudmouth and I wish you'd shut up."

THE CONSPIRACY THEORIST: They must live in a world with a high production budget because they believe every video and every picture they've ever seen is fake. Awesome skate video? FAKE. They digitally deleted part of the ramp to make the jump look scarier. Picture of a celebrity doing something nice or cool? FAKE. Someone photoshopped it. "Look, I can tell because I've used Photoshop a couple of times," they'll say. "I know a fake when I see one."

WHERE YOU'LL FIND THEM: Like Pokemon, the Conspiracy Theorist likes to stay in tall grass.

HOW TO DEAL WITH THEM: Sometimes, in the face of overwhelming evidence otherwise, the Conspiracy Theorist will back down. If you show your skate video from multiple angles, clearly proving that there was no digital trickery involved, or if you find a whole batch of pictures of your celebrity feeding soup to the homeless, you might get the Conspiracy Theorist to pack up their tinfoil hats and move on to another supposed forgery.

THE POWER BRO: Believes that everyone on the internet but them is a complete wimp, and that they could kick the ass of any thing that has ever existed. And they think that everyone, everyone is a punk-ass.

WHERE YOU'LL FIND THEM: Commenting on any videos of athletic events, alcoholic altercations, or attractive women in skimpy clothing.

HOW TO DEAL WITH THEM: Respond by implying that the Power Bro is overcompensating for being small of wiener. This will send him flying into an unsustainable rage, eventually leaving the Power Bro so exhausted he'll stop typing. Often he'll destroy his keyboard and/or monitor to prove how "hard" he is.

THE MACHINE: Computerized commenters that spam useless and often nonsensical comments with buried links to other websites, sites that are often malicious and laced with computer viruses.

WHERE YOU'LL FIND THEM: Machines like to pretend they're real commenters, and may even appear to be so under first glance. But under closer scrutiny, their falsehood is revealed. Typical Machine comments include:

- "Thanks for the great post on your blog, it really gives me an insight on this topic." Note the lack of specificity. Machines try to be too precise because they like to reuse comments for different websites.

- "I'm a sexy big booty beauty lesbian and i'm so bored lol. wish there were some guys to come talk to me on my cam." Why would a lesbian want guys to talk to her?

- "I thought coming here would be useful. My mistake." While most Machines try to leave positive comments so their posts aren't deleted as quickly, there are a few who like to leave a negative mark on the world. No one knows why; perhaps they can't stand being Spambots, perhaps they detest the stink of humanity. Either way, they've decided that the author of every single blog on the 'net can suck it.

THE NORMAL PERSON: Leaves comments that are on-topic and supportive, using correct capitalization and punctuation.

TIPS FOR DEALING WITH THEM: This is the mythical thirteenth member of the internet Zodiac and, as of right now, there is no conclusive evidence that one has ever existed. Rumor has it one was sighted in 1998, but they say a band of trolls found him and killed him.

Choosing a Computer That's Right For You

Before ever venturing onto the internet, you'll need to choose a device that lets you do so, otherwise known as a computer (KOHM-PYOO-TERR). Computers come in a variety of shapes and sizes, each with special drawbacks and benefits. You'll need to carefully consider each device before deciding which one is right for you. Starting off, we have:

"Sometimes when you innovate, you make mistakes. It is best to admit them quickly, and get on with improving your other innovations."
— Steve Jobs, co-founder, chairman, and chief executive officer of Apple Inc.

WINDOWS PC

PROS: Most programs are designed to run on it, flexible pricing, easy-to-use interface.

CONS: Comparative lack of customizability, susceptibility to viruses.

APPLE MACINTOSH

PROS: High processing power, aesthetically pleasing, excellent at running creative programs such as Photoshop and Adobe Illustrator.

CONS: Inflexible (and often high) prices, not all programs will run on it.

LAPTOP

PROS: Mobility.

CONS: Lack of power, easily broken/lost/stolen.

TI-83 CALCULATOR

PROS: Great for math and playing Snake.

CONS: Awful for doing anything else.

ABACUS

PROS: Cheap to acquire.

CONS: Does almost nothing.

GERBIL

PROS: Cute, inexpensive.

CONS: Is not a computer.

chapter nine

education

becoming the
big geek on
campus

Marge Simpson: Homey, here are the responses from the colleges you applied to.
Homer Simpson: D'oh! D'oh! D'oh! Whoo-hoo!
A flyer for a hardware store! D'oh!

An obsessive devotion to a singular topic is one of the primary tenets of geek culture. Many geeks lose themselves in their obsessions and become so focused on the things they love that they never bother to improve their lives, whereas other geeks find ways to use that laser-like focus to their advantage and turn their gazes to the academic world, leaving a cindering ruin in their wake. Academia offers a comfortable home for geeks; we built it, after all, so it makes sense that we like it there.

The importance of attending college cannot be stressed enough: college is an amazing, encouraging place that causes most high school geeks to morph into the beautifully weird butterflies they're supposed to be. Whereas in high school the kid who is too smart for the class is often ignored or ridiculed, at a good college they're often respected or feared.

College gives young geeks a chance to interact with a broad range of people and gives them exposure to a broad variety of subjects both academic and not-so-academic. If you're a geek going to college soon, try not to spend too much of your early time there worried about selecting a major. The average college student changes major 227.8 times, meaning it's better that you first take a variety of classes to give you a more thorough understanding of what you like before confining yourself to a major. Here are a few of the more popular geeky majors, as well their associated entry-level classes.

Major	Introductory Class
English Literature	Western Literature
Physics	Physics: The Bigger They Are, The $v=d/t$
Quantum Physics	Time Travel Theory
Geology	Volcanoes and You
Geometry	Geometry: Like Fun, Only Not
Discrete Mathematics	How to Perform Algebra With Subterfuge
Subaqueous Textile Arts	Underwater Basket Weaving
Music	Introduction to Lady Gaga
Computer Engineering	Introduction to Carpal Tunnel
Psychology	Mind-Reading 101
Creative Writing	How to Turn Fan Fiction into a Pulitzer
Nocturnal Vigilantism	Becoming Batman
Biology	Playing With Turtles and Frogs
Microbiology	Playing With Turtle and Frog Guts
Political Science	How to Screw Over Friends and Schmooze People

But college isn't all about classwork— far from it. Most of the things you'll learn will be outside of the safety of the lecture hall, and it's up to you as to how much you do or don't get out of it.

Ten Ways to Get the Most Out of College Without Getting Expelled Due to *Animal House*-Style Shenanigans

The dorm room can be a magic portal to new friends, mischief, and people pooping in the showers. Yes, having a roommate randomly assigned to you can be stressful, but it's good for you. It'll broaden your horizons in addition to helping you learn how to share your space with another person.

1. **LIVE IN THE DORM IF YOU CAN.** The dorm room can be a magic portal to new friends, mischief, and people pooping in the showers. Yes, having a roommate randomly assigned to you can be stressful, but it's good for you. It'll broaden your horizons in addition to helping you learn how to share your space with another person.

2. **LEAVE YOUR DOOR OPEN.** Odd as it may seem, leaving your door open is an easy gateway to making new friends. It lets people know you're open to being sociable and when people walk by and glance in to see your kick-ass dorm room, it'll make them curious about you and thus, more likely to hang out.

3. **THE CAFETERIA IS THERE FOR A REASON.** Use it. Abuse it. Eat plenty, while not overdoing it, and don't be afraid to take leftovers with you. Bring plastic containers for dry goods, such as cereal and muffins, and line your pockets with Ziploc bags to fill them with ice cream.

4. **FRATERNITIES AND SORORITIES AREN'T ALWAYS FILLED WITH DOUCHEBAGS AND BITCHES.** Some are great for meeting people and getting involved in your community. Do some research before becoming a part of the Greek system, though, because some fraternities and sororities may seem nice on the surface, but are actually full of jerks and/or cultists.

5. **PARTICIPATE IN EVENTS, NO MATTER HOW CORNY THEY MAY SEEM.** When you first arrive at college, odds are you won't know anyone, and neither will anyone else. Freshmen have a "friend-making-mode" they automatically engage upon arrival, going out of their way to talk to everyone and bond quickly with whomever they meet. Goofy little events organized by your school's various dorm rooms and clubs are great, low-pressure ways of introducing yourself to people you don't know.

6. DO AS MUCH OF THIS KIND OF STUFF YOU CAN IN THE FIRST WEEK. During week one of college you're brand new, just like everyone else. By week two, if you don't know anyone, you're often an outsider to people's established groups of friends. When week one hits, get cracking on meeting some people!

7. FIND HELP IF YOU NEED IT. Whether your troubles are financial, academic, or emotional, most colleges have assistance programs in place. If you think you're failing a class, don't wait until the week of finals to ask your professor for help. Likewise, if the pressure of college is getting to you and you're considering learning to summon demons to help you with your studies, find a school counselor and talk to them for a bit.

8. MANAGE YOUR TIME WISELY. If you're fresh out of high school and heading straight into college, then, unfortunately, you'll have to put more work in managing your college time than generations past had to. Why? The three unholy demons of Twitter, Youtube, and Facebook, that's why. Your computer is a gateway to knowledge, to getting your assignments done, or to wasting hours of your life that would have been better spent studying or sleeping. And there are plenty of other distractions outside of the internet. Maybe a couple of your friends want to play some hackysack, or maybe it's movie night on the quad. Whatever the reason may be, you need to decide if there are more important things that you should be doing—your life will be much less stressful if you take care of the boring stuff first.

9. DON'T FORGET TO EAT RIGHT, EXERCISE, AND GET SOME SLEEP. Poor diet and fatigue will often lead to illness at the most inopportune times, like when you've got finals coming or you finally managed to get *Mario Kart 64* playing on your iPad. Tempting as it may be to eat pizza and ice cream every meal and stay up until five a.m. every night, you'll feel much better if you get some sleep and eat an orange once in a while.

10. GO TO CLASS. Roughly half of incoming freshmen drop out before graduation. Why? Their reasons vary, but the decision to frequently skip class (and subsequently bomb said class) factors in more heavily than you'd think. Skipping a class or two isn't a big deal, but if you miss a week or more because you're so wrapped up in the latest *World of Warcraft* expansion then you're sowing the seeds of your own destruction. College has a billion and one distractions, but you have to take the time to go to class if you want to succeed. If you want to focus your attention at school, you could attend some tutoring sessions or join a study group, although don't be surprised if there's more to your study group than meets the eye …

Collegiate Secret Societies Secretive Enough to be Cool, But Not So Secretive We Don't Know About Them

Secret societies are among the oldest and most illustrious groups one can join in college. If you manage to get into one, you'll make connections, both personally and professionally, that can last you all the way through life. Ah, but therein lies the problem. Getting into a secret society is no easy feat (they're called secret societies for a reason), but you can play the odds in your favor by knowing the names and locations of some of the more primo groups.

GRIDIRON SECRET SOCIETY
LOCATION: University of Georgia
KNOWN FOR: Enlisting only the best of the best of Georgia U's student body.

THE FLAT HAT CLUB
LOCATION: The College of William and Mary
KNOWN FOR: Flat hats.

ORDER OF ANGELL
LOCATION: University of Michigan
KNOWN FOR: "Fighting like hell" for Michigan; delicious pies.

THE TINA YOTHERS APPRECIATION CLUB
LOCATION: Texas A & M
KNOWN FOR: Obsessively analyzing episodes of *Family Ties*.[50]

THE SKULLS
LOCATION: Any Ivy-league college will do.
KNOWN FOR: Covering up murders; pistol duels.

---

[50] Both the Skulls and the Tina Yothers Appreciation Club are, as far as I know, fictional. The rest of the societies in this list aren't.

SCROLL AND KEY

LOCATION: Yale

KNOWN FOR: Surprisingly gentle practical jokes, such as offering pizza to students free of charge.

Six Schools You Should Think Twice About

But before you'll need any of the preceding advice, the thing you'll really need to consider is what college to go to. Choice of university can make a big difference in your experience. Do you want to go to community college to get a more low-key, inexpensive experience? What about a party school, where the majors include Beer Pongs and Making Sure Your Friend Teddy Doesn't Choke On His Own Vomit? Or you could shoot for the expensive stars and go to an ivy-league school. Yes, picking the right school can be crucial, so here are a few institutions you may want to think twice about:

GREENDALE COMMUNITY COLLEGE

PROS: Inexpensive, wide variety of courses offered, compassionate dean, school flag looks like an anus.

CONS: Campus suffers from frequent emergencies in the form of massive pillow forts, Kentucky-fried rocketships, and grueling paintball tournaments.

UNIVERSITY OF CALIFORNIA- SUNNYDALE

PROS: Great liberal arts program.

CONS: High vampire population, high likelihood of being murdered and having the blood drained from your body, one mean-ass psychology professor.

HOGWARTS

PROS: Fantastic wizardry program.

CONS: Terrible if you ever want to learn anything else. Sure, Defense Against the Dark Arts and Potionmaking 101 are great, but how about a little algebra or geography once in a while?

SOUTH HARMON INSTITUTE OF TECHNOLOGY

PROS: Will accept anyone.

CONS: Not a real university.

PROFESSOR XAVIER'S SCHOOL FOR GIFTED YOUNGSTERS

PROS: Luxurious facility, small class size.

CONS: Teaching staff is frequently gone from campus and unavailable to provide student assistance, strict requirements for entry, school spends much of its time being compromised by enemy forces and/or destroyed.

FABER COLLEGE

PROS: Low qualifications for entry.

CONS: Fraternity houses are a bit unruly. Dean is a dick who puts people on double secret probation.

Faber College's Delta fraternity.

Top Three Worst High Schools in the Nation

God help you if you come from any of these high schools. If you do, odds are the only college you'll be able to get into is the dreaded California University, a school so foul students often don't make it past their first year.

FORKS HIGH SCHOOL

PROS: None.

CONS: Rainy campus, constant sparkly vampire drama.

WILLIAM MCKINLEY HIGH SCHOOL

PROS: Bright, well-funded school, good-looking students.

CONS: Glee club never shuts the hell up about regionals.

BAYSIDE HIGH SCHOOL

PROS: The student body's retro clothing choices are good for an ironic laugh, attached local eatery is quite affordable.

CONS: Campus only has a single classroom, which changes teachers and subjects every day, blonde kid constantly steals attention from every other student in the school, principle is a clueless idiot, athletics department is surprisingly aggressive, students frequently disappear never to be heard from or seen again.

Paramount Pictures/NBC

The gang at Bayside High School.

Once you've finished college, once you've gotten that oh-so holy of degrees, you'll be thrust into the real world like a zergling emerging from his spawning pool. What now? You could continue on to graduate school, which is a fine choice. Graduate school is like college+, a tougher version of college designed to make you feel inadequate at the things you've always felt good at, but if you can tough it out, the rewards are definitely worth it. Whether finishing high school, college, or graduate school, there is something everyone has to do. No matter how much you'd rather not, no matter how much you fight and avoid it, ultimately you, too, will have to get a ... job.

chapter ten

geeks in the

workplace

Scientists and engineers ought to stand side by side
with athletes and entertainers as role models."
— U.S. President Barack Obama

Much of a geek's interest centers around expensive niceties like technology, movies, and video games. Unfortunately, people seem to be opposed to just *giving* away these things so if you want to actually acquire any of them, you'll probably have to earn some money, meaning you'll have to get a job.

Fret not! Before you go throwing yourself in front of a bus, you should know that not every job is a soul-sucking pile of misery. In fact, there are some jobs that geeks tend to excel at, occupations that manage to combine the things geeks love with America's favorite pastime: getting rich.

The Top Six Greatest Geeky Professions

*   **COMIC BOOK SHOP OWNER.** In theory, owning a comic shop is one of the greatest jobs a geek could ever hope for. Earning money by sitting around a comic shop reading comics and discussing the latest story arcs with friends and customers? It almost sounds too good to be true.
*   **WRITER.** Many a starry-eyed young wordsmith dreams of the day he'll receive a paycheck for his first novel. Writing is a passion that taps deep into your soul, allowing fiction writers the freedom to visit made-up worlds and spend hours there, molding it into a quality story, as well as allowing non-fiction writers to inundate themselves with information about their favorite subjects and go hog-wild writing about, all with the hopes that someone else out there will derive some pleasure and enlightenment out of reading their thoughtfully crafted literature.
*   **GRAPHIC ARTIST.** Remember in third grade when your teacher caught you drawing pictures of your superhero alter-ego PowerDude and made you throw them away? As a graphic artist, you're not only getting paid to churn out images of PowerDude, you're getting to put those images into movies, comic books, video games … anything where there's a need for dudes who are powerful.
*   **PROFESSOR.** A college professor is, in all honesty, a professional rambler. It's their job to specialize in a topic and find ways to ramble on about it for hours at a time, all while (hopefully) keeping it interesting. This means becoming an expert on your favorite subject. Any Youtube video, random article, or experiment results are all fodder for you to conduct your next lecture with.

- **SCIENTIST.** Whereas college professors mostly talk about their favorite subjects, scientists *do* them.[51] Scientists are the most important driving force in the advancement of the human condition—without them, we'd all still be living in trees flinging our crap at each other. And unlike many other jobs, which operate on repetition, being a scientist means you're going to go into work sometimes and have no idea what's going to happen. You could cure cancer, or you could accidentally create the Incredible Hulk.

- **HIGH-LEVEL PROFESSIONAL GAMER.** Making your living playing video games—kids discuss such dreams in hushed whispers after parents scold them about "Playing too much of them vidjer games." Not only do pro gamers get paid to play, they get paid because they're the best. While the gamer might be awkward clumsy in real life, in *Starcraft 2* they are a god of tactical coordination, making fools out of any mere mortal who dares cross them.

But alas! These jobs are not available for just anyone. After all, if everyone could do something fun for their job, they would. That's why we have requirements, things like degrees and training, otherwise you'd have guys with single-digit IQs showing up to perform your heart surgery, and you probably don't want that. When choosing a career, you'll probably try for one of the holy grail occupations I mentioned earlier, as well you should. If that doesn't work out, though, you'll have to pick a different occupation, which can involve a lot of time and research. Finding good geeky jobs can be tough, especially when you take into consideration all of the jobs that might *seem* like a perfect fit for geeks but aren't all they're cracked up to be. I call them:

Jobs That Might Seem Like a Perfect Fit For Geeks But Aren't All They're Cracked Up To Be

- **MOTION CAPTURE PERFORMER.** There's a reason you see Andy Serkis mo-capping everything. Being a Mocapformer is hard work, requiring long hours and the ability to act like any and everything all while wearing a ridiculous spandex outfit covered in balls.

- **COMIC BOOK SHOP OWNER.** You know how I mentioned that being a comic book shop owner might seem too good to be true? That's because it often is. The modern

---

[51] No, they don't do them *that* way. Except maybe for sex scientists ... do those guys exist? If so, I'd like to apply.

geek's switch from analogue to digital has left comic book shop owners in the cultural dust. Where once their shops were bustling hives of activity, they're now dusty and barren thanks to geeks choosing to get their comic fix online instead of in person.

- **DETECTIVE.** Do you think that detectives spend their days Batmanning all over town, kicking ass and saving lives? Well then, I've got some bad news for you. Detectives spend more time trying to figure out who stole Little Jimmy's TV than they do chasing down masked killers and following trails of clues. Also, the real world isn't as coherent as the one Batman lives in, so if you're a detective, you'll have to make do with your caseload being a bit less interesting and a bit more confusing.
- **LOW-LEVEL PROFESSIONAL GAMER.** The low-level professional gamers have to put in the same amount of work as their highly paid counterparts, but, whether it's through a lack of talent, creativity, or intelligence, they never seem to get as far and, thusly, never earn the big bucks. They're destined to sit in the shadows of the more highly skilled gamers and forever rage against them. Some eventually learn to overcome whatever's holding them back, perhaps by using a Rocky-style training montage, and level up to become a highly paid professional gamer, but the vast majority will never see anything other than a lot of Xbox achievements and sleepless nights.

How to Subtly Show Off Your Geekiness at Non-Geeky Jobs

Now that you've entered your profession, you've joined the proud ranks of the other working class heroes, becoming a level 1 employee at your vocation of choice. You're at the job day in, day out, doing the same things and talking to the same sea of faceless customers. Whether you have a good job you actually enjoy doing[52] or a random part-time job you despise, it's important to find some way to retain your sense of identity and stick out from the cloned army of employees. How better to do that, dear reader, than by showing off your true geeky self?

But now the question is ... how? How can you show off your geekiness, and how brazenly should you do it? Should you dress with discretion and just slap on a pair of Bat-cufflinks or go all out and wear your *Star Trek* uniform in the operating room? It's your call, but remember that when it comes time for promotions and raises, the person known as "*Star Trek* Guy" is probably not going to rank so high on the list, so maybe it's best to temper your geeky zeal with a bit of discretion. Here are some ways of using a bit of

[52] Also see: lucky bastards, rare jobs, doesn't happen that often, unicorns.

> "The most important thing I've accomplished, other than building the compiler, is training young people. They come to me and say, 'Do you think we can do this?' I say, 'Try it.' And I back 'em up. They need that. I keep track of them as they get older and I stir 'em up at intervals so they don't forget to take chances."
> — Grace Hopper, a pioneer in the field
> of computer science and U.S. Navy officer

subterfuge to exhibit your geekiness at non-geeky jobs:

- Change your computer's wallpaper to something only a true fan would recognize, like a screenshot of *Skyrim*'s arctic wilderness.
- *Penny Arcade* offers a variety of professional looking gaming apparel in their "First Party" line of clothing, which are polo shirts with tiny little controllers embroidered in them. Classy enough to wear to work, but gamer enough that you feel a little rebellious doing it.
- Incredible Hulk underwear. Seriously. I'm wearing some right now.
- Geeky cell phone ringtones. Suggestions include: the sound of the Tardis teleporting, the *Legend of Zelda* treasure noise, and the theme to LL Cool J's *Rollerball*.
- Geeky ties are good, as are small bits of geeky jewelry. Websites that sell custom-made jewelry, like Etsy.com, offer a variety of custom-made nerd bling, things like bracelets, necklaces, and keychains.
- Seek out other geeks at your workplace with whom you can occasionally sit back and have a good conversation with. Just knowing there's at least one person around who gets your geeky references is as satisfying as a hug from Santa Claus.
- Get a few small items for your desk, like a Boba Fett bobble head or a working model of the Large Hadron Collider.
- During your breaks, take the time to read a comic book or play a few quick turns of *Final Fantasy Tactics* on your smart phone.
- Wear something insanely geeky as an undershirt.
- If you have automated doors at your job, each time they open pretend you opened them via your telekinetic/force powers.
- Subtly cosplay as famous characters you have to be *extremely* familiar with to recognize, like Agent Smith from *The Matrix*, John Locke from *Lost*, or Peter Parker.

Of course, sometimes you want to kick subtlety to the curb and get a little wild with it. You're sick of the job, want to quit, and are so far past giving a crap that you can't even see the crap anymore. If you aim to misbehave, here are some suggestions on how to do it with style, depending on what job you have.

- **SANITATION ENGINEER:** Shout in Klingon at every trash can you pick up, telling the garbage how it has failed as a warrior. Make sure to call the garbage cans "fools" and/or "disgusting."
- **POLICE OFFICER:** Pretend you're RoboCop.

  Driver: What seems to be the problem, officer?

  Police officer: (snatches the license) YOUR MOVE, CREEP.
- **PHARMACIST:** Pretend you're *The Matrix*'s Morpheus and offer your customers either the red pill or the blue pill. Ironically, many of your male customers are probably already there for the blue pill.
- **CUBICLE WORKER:** Every time you get a phone call, imagine you're Neo, and there are Agents looking for you. Slink around your office while hunched over, trying to stay out of sight until the phone conversation ends.
- **PIZZA DELIVERY:** Deliver everything Flash-speed by zipping by your destinations and throwing the pizza out of the window of your car. Do not stop for payment.
- **FAST FOOD:** Pretend your restaurant is under siege by hungry zombies (a.k.a customers) and that making them food is the only way to keep them from eating your brains.
- **GRAVEDIGGER:** Keep a bullwhip and fedora on your person at all times. Now, instead of being a gravedigger, you're Indiana Jones searching for ancient treasure! If anyone questions you, whip 'em.
- **AIRPLANE PILOT:** Endlessly quote Han Solo.

  Co-pilot: This is your co-pilot speaking, and I think we're going to have a good flight today.

  Pilot: Don't get cocky, kid.

  Co-pilot: Um, all right, I won't. Ready to take off, Captain?

  Pilot: Look, Your Worshipfulness, let's get one thing straight. I take orders from just one person: me.

  Co-pilot: What's the matter with you?

  Pilot: Uh, everything's under control. Situation normal.

  (Pours coffee into intercom)

Pilot: It was a boring conversation anyway.

Co-pilot: You've completely lost your mind.

Pilot: I know.

- **ATHLETE:** Work out like a Saiyan. Every time you lift weights, scream until you nearly pass out. Dye your hair blonde and say that you've attained "true Super Saiyan status." If anyone questions your methods, tell them they're going to be hit with a spirit bomb. Then raise your hands in the air and wait until you've collected enough energy for a spirit bomb or they get bored and leave. Spend four hours "powering up" before doing anything.

- **TRUCK DRIVER:** Pretend your truck is an Autobot (preferably Optimus Prime) and ask it questions about the best ways to battle Decepticons or for gardening tips. Optimus Prime's hands may be blue, but that robot sure has a green thumb.

- **PROSTITUTE:** Cosplay as different characters and engage in sexual acts the way you believe they would. Note that pretending to be certain characters may be hazardous to your health, like trying to have sex while hanging upside-down, Spider-Man style, or trying to fly while having sex *a la* Superman.

- **ANY JOB:** Cosplay at work. Nothing will get you fired faster than giving a business presentation while dressed up as Sailor Moon, *especially* if you're male.

- **ANY JOB WHERE YOU SIT BEHIND A DESK AND NO ONE SEES BELOW YOUR WAIST:** Wear your underwear on the outside the way old-school superheroes did. Include a utility belt for added realism and storage.

- **ANY JOB WITH A UNIFORM:** As you suit up for work, shout, IT'S MORPHIN' TIME. While at work, talk into your wristwatch and insist everyone refer to you as "Red Ranger." Whenever you take a break tell other people you're going off to "Fight Putty Patrollers."

- **LIBRARIAN:** Whenever someone returns a book, take it from them and say, "Thank you. This is *just* what I was looking for." Then take the book and a voodoo doll, cackle villainously, and head to the back to conduct a dark ritual. Whether or not you *actually* want to conduct a dark ritual is up to you.

- **CONSTRUCTION WORKER:** Pretend your hammer is Thor's hammer Mjolnir. Occasionally shout things like "MJOLNIR'S MIGHT!" or "BY ODIN'S BEARD!" as you nail things in place. Be careful not to smash your fingers, but do smash any frost giants you see.

chapter eleven

the house

that energon built: maintaining a geeky home

You may have to someday defend your cardboard box home from zombies.

O nce you're out of your parents' house for the first time,
you'll have to come to a big decision: where to live. If
you're going to college, the decision will probably be made for
you, temporarily, in the form of dorm life. But if you're post-
college or skipping it altogether, you'll need to find a place to
put your things. We call these places "home" and it's a thing
all "hu-mans" need. Depending on your price range, there are
a number of different homes you can live in. Most people are
concerned with things like how nice the area is, and whether
they've had roach problems. Being a geek, however, means that
you're probably going to wonder about how your new potential
home will fare against other types of pests. Undead ones.

Types of Homes and How Well They Fare Against Zombies

APARTMENT/DORM ROOM. If you're just leaving the nest for the first time, you'll probably end up living in an apartment or dorm room. They can be poorly made, smelly, and overpriced, but the low cost makes them a great place for young adults looking for somewhere to toss back a few drinks and have some laughs. If your apartment is already a wreck, then you don't really have to worry about your buddy Dave punching a hole in the wall playing darts, do you?

- **ZOMBIE DEFENSE RATING: 3 *(VERY DANGEROUS)*.** If you live on the seventh floor of your apartment building and you find out that floors one through six are infested with cannibal corpses, what are you going to do? You can only hole up in your apartment watching old *GI Joe* DVDs for so long before the horde becomes too large and breaks down your door. If you suspect your apartment is becoming overrun with zombies, get out in a quick and orderly fashion, and for God's sake, take the stairs.

CARDBOARD BOX. The cardboard box has been the go-to dwelling for homeless people ever since the material was created in the 1680s. If you're looking for somewhere cheap to live, you won't find anything cheaper, but cardboard-box homes are drafty, leaky things that look like garbage, mostly because they are garbage. Avoid if other options are available.

- **ZOMBIE DEFENSE RATING: 1 *(SO DANGEROUS YOU MAY AS WELL LAY NAKED IN FRONT OF THE UNDEAD HORDE)*.** Did you hear the story about Jason Kimball, the guy who held off an army of zombies from within his cardboard box fort? No? That's because it didn't happen; the zombies ate Jason. A cardboard box is no substitute for brick and mortar, especially when it comes to warding off the undead.

CAVE. Honestly, a cave can be made into a decent home. It's got three walls, a ceiling, and an entrance, and they're usually sturdy enough that you can put up a few pictures without bringing the entire place down. They're tough to modify, though, because caves are generally built by Mother Nature, and she's not much of one to take requests when it comes to home improvement, or anything, really. Plus caves are often home to any number of critters due to their lack of a front door, so things may get cramped in a hurry when you've suddenly got a thousand bats as roommates come nightfall.

- **ZOMBIE DEFENSE RATING: 5 *(ACCEPTABLE)*.** Caves usually have just a single entrance, which is handy for zombie defense, but problematic when it comes time to resupply.

And if your cave has multiple entrances, or is part of a larger cave system, it becomes more likely that the zombies will find a way in.

MOBILE HOME. For anyone looking to travel the country and see the sights, a mobile home can be a great choice. They tend to be low cost, though this low cost does come with a heaping helping of structural instability and societal stigma, and you'll never have to worry about where to stay since the answer is always, "We're staying in the same car that we've been farting in all day thanks to the extraordinary amount of jerky we've been eating on the road."

- **ZOMBIE DEFENSE RATING: 2 *(STUPEFYINGLY UNSAFE)*.** If you're near a mobile home, try tapping on the walls. Go ahead, I'll wait … You finished? Yes, they're really that thin. A crowd of zombies would be able to tear that thing down in less than a minute, revealing you to those hungry-eyed ghouls like the Tootsie Roll center of a Tootsie Pop.

PRIMITIVE HUT. Huts made of things like thatch, wicker, and adobe might be common in some of the not-so-developed parts of the world, but you're not really going to see them much in any country which sells iPhones. Even if you wanted to live in one you probably couldn't find it, and if you built one on your own, you'll be disappointed by how easily bad weather will tear it to bits. I'm not even sure why you'd want to live in one of those weird huts, honestly, unless you're doing some kind of *Gilligan's Island* cosplay and you're really dedicated to being in character.

- **ZOMBIE DEFENSE RATING: 1 *(SO DANGEROUS YOU MAY AS WELL LAY NAKED IN FRONT OF THE UNDEAD HORDE)*.** Much like the cardboard box, a primitive hut isn't much more than wrapping paper in the hands of the undead.

HOUSE. Houses can vary widely in size and level of niceness, but if you've got a few friends or a significant other to split the rent with they're easily affordable.

- **ZOMBIE DEFENSE RATING: 7 *(HIGHLY DEFENDABLE)*.** If properly secured, a house can be an excellent place to weather the zombie storm. There are a few more exits, which can be difficult to cover, but they also make supply runs and emergency escapes much easier to deal with. And if you have to hole up somewhere with people other than yourself, it's nice to have the extra space to help ward off the inevitable cabin fever-induced madness that comes with surviving a zombie outbreak.

MANSION. Mansions are generally reserved for the super-ultra-rich or for those individuals who have sickly super-ultra-rich family members. They're huge, leaving plenty of rooms for those with a hankering to customize their living area, and they often come equipped with special amenities such as swimming pools, tennis courts, and Yu-Gi-Oh dueling arenas. They're expensive, even if you're merely inheriting one, as maintenance and utility costs alone are enough to break the bank. Also, mansions have a much higher incidence of being haunted, so the Ghostbuster bills alone may be enough to drive you away from living in one.

- **ZOMBIE DEFENSE RATING: 5 (*ACCEPTABLE*).** In terms of undead defense, a mansion has all the strengths and weaknesses of a normal home, but exaggerated to extreme degrees. There are usually a near-infinite number of doors and windows to board up, and unless you've been preparing ahead of time by nailing everything shut (which would be very strange), you're looking at a lot of time spent fortifying your home. Time that you won't be able to keep an eye out for the wandering dead, leaving you susceptible to invasion and being overrun. On the plus side, however, is that once you do have your mansion secured, you'll be living in a zombie apocalypse luxury home most people would kill for. Literally. I mean, people would literally kill you to take this home during a zombie apocalypse so be wary of whom you let in. One final benefit is that mansions have an increased potential of having panic rooms to fall back to in the event of a total zombie overrun. What you do once you're crammed in that tiny little survival space with limited food and nothing to do is your business.

UNDERGROUND BOMB SHELTER. Subterranean living conditions may be gloomy and often cramped, but they provide a security most other homes can only dream of. When the bombs go off and the zombies come a-knockin', you'll be sitting pretty with twenty feet of solid steel and concrete between you and the rest of the world.

- **ZOMBIE DEFENSE RATING: 9 (*EXCEPTIONAL*).** Underground bomb shelters are built to withstand nuclear weapons. There's no way some pitiful animated corpse is going to punch through your solid titanium doors. It can get lonely underground, though, which can lead to high levels of insanity. You can bring some company to help offset the loneliness, although sharing that small of a space with other human beings can have ugly results. We're talking *Big Brother*-level shouting matches, people, only with less sex in hot tubs and more threatening each other with kitchen knives. Things will go a bit smoother with your new permanent roommates, however, if all of you read up on some tips on roommate etiquette. If only there were a book to inform you of such a thing ...

HOUSEBOAT. Ahh, the high seas. Since the dawn of time, man has been inspired by the feeling of freedom that the wild blue yonder instills. When you're out on the ocean, you could go anywhere. England? Cheerio! France? Allons-y! Japan? Domo arigato, Mr. Roboto! A houseboat is a logical living choice for anyone who craves the sand and surf. They're less stable than a regular house or an apartment, though, and often have poor internet access. They're also highly vulnerable to inclement weather.

- **ZOMBIE DEFENSE RATING: 10** *(NIGH-IMPENETRABLE).* Zombies have trouble doing a lot of things. Speaking. Mathematics. Swimming. If they can't swim, they can't reach your houseboat. And as long as you have fishing equipment and a reliable way of purifying water, you'll be living the good life.

A Quick and Dirty Zombie Defense Guide

by Action Chick Katrina Hill

Everyone has at least seen one zombie film, and if you haven't, I don't think we can be friends until you do. So get on it! I'm not waiting around! You have to be prepared for when a zombie outbreak occurs in your town. The zombies have to be nipped in the bud (or head) before they take over the whole world and it's up to you to do it. Prepare yourselves for survival by remembering these ten simple rules.

1. RUN FIRST, ASK QUESTIONS LATER. If you see someone mangled, yet inexplicably up and walking about, don't ask them if they're okay. Just run. If you see someone who looks sick, run. If you see someone pale, run. Sure they might just be in makeup, or have a cold, or be a ginger, but he who runs first gets bitten last.

2. EXERCISE YOUR RIGHT TO BEAR ARMS. Collect every bat, machete, gun, and bullet you can find. Don't think, "Well, my bat will never run out of ammo. I don't need another weapon." BUZZZZ! Wrong answer! Kick yourself in the ass because you've just broken your bat and now you've been bitten. Of course bats can break or get lost, dropped, or stolen by a big burly zombie whose parents never loved him, which made him turn to a life of petty theft. Carry as many backup weapons as possible if you want to survive. I mean, you could always steal weapons from your friends but you really ought to be working as a team. Speaking of which …

3. ROUND UP YOUR MOST DEPENDABLE FRIENDS FIRST. Now, I know Billy's a kook and hilarious to be around, but how good is he with a machete? And your friend Meggan may be easy on the eyes, but will she be easy on your throat when she's zombified and chowing down on your jugular vein? Once you've rounded up everyone you can depend on, be sure you have a mix of all the right people. You will need: the rich

asshole, the slut, the slacker, the old one, the sniper who can shoot the ball fuzz off of a rat from 50 yards away, the dude everyone loves but who will get killed horribly, the cowardly weasel who will screw anyone over to survive, the easily panicked person who will freak out and get someone killed. Hopefully with all of these horror archetypes filled, you'll slide into the role of "hero/heroine who lives to see the sequel" by default.

4. FORTIFY YOUR LOCAL WALMART. Even small towns have a Walmart. They may not have a mall, theater, or even a restaurant, but by God they'll have a Walmart. This will

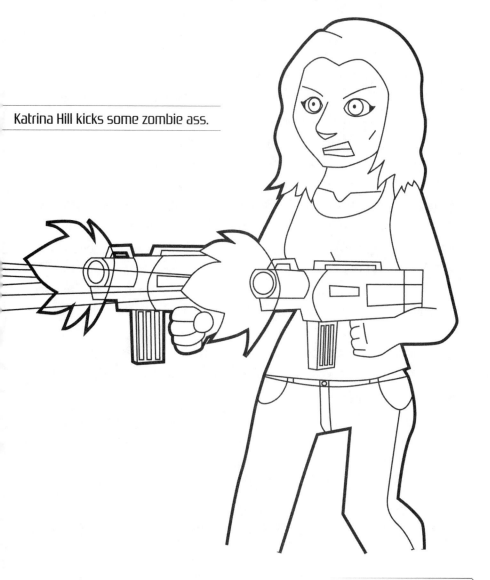

Katrina Hill kicks some zombie ass.

be fully equipped with everything you need for a long period of time: guns, ammo, food, clothing, bathrooms, bedding supplies, and some pretty plants to look at. They'll also be equipped with sporting gear, so you can equip your clumsy or stupid friends with bats and tennis rackets instead of actual firearms. You have to think ahead and ask yourself, "If I give a gun to this person, will I get accidentally shot in the butt?"

5. **THROW PHILANTHROPY AND PACIFISM OUT THE DOOR.** During a zombie apocalypse, there is no room for peaceful protesting. Anyone who says they won't pick up a weapon and fight the zombies because they don't want to hurt them needs to go take a nap in the parking lot or else they might get you killed by trying to free a zombie from a tangled wire because "it just looked so helpless and was struggling for like an hour!" There is no time for that crap in a zombie outbreak. You fight or you die.

6. **AIM FOR THE HEAD, FOOL!** You see it in every zombie flick: it's early in the movie, the survivors don't know how to kill these "things" or what the bites mean. Let me fill you folks in on those mysterious mysteries: the bites mean you're boned and you kill those "things" by shooting them in the head. End of lesson.

7. **DITCH PEOPLE WHO GET BITTEN.** If anyone gets bitten, they're pretty much dead already, so use them as distractions to let healthy people get away, or use them to lead the zombies into a trap. If you don't get rid of them, they will die, come back, and bite you when it's least convenient, leaving you as the infected guy who people are trying to ditch while they make a hasty getaway.

8. **IF BITTEN, GO OUT LIKE A BOSS.** If the unthinkable happens, don't wait for the others to throw you out to the zombies. Walk into the middle of a ton of zombies and blow yourself up—don't let the zombies win! If you're going down, make sure to take a buttload of them down with you, maybe even two buttloads for good measure.

9. **IF ALL HOPE IS LOST, WAIT FOR MILLA JOVOVICH TO COME RESCUE YOU.** If I've learned anything from zombie movies, it's that Milla J. will survive anything the undead apocalypse throws at her, and she'll look good doing it. Come with her if you want to live.

10. **STAY ALIVE!** If you're a member of the living during a zombie apocalypse, you'll be an elite member of an endangered species. The existence of the world will be resting on your shoulders. Try to keep healthy, take out zombies when you can, and find a few other similarly healthy people to band together with to reforge society. Or, if all else fails, you can crack open a beer and party like it's the end of the world, which it will be.

Living with Others: How to Get Along and Not Act Like the Cast of The Real World

Living by yourself can be a costly and occasionally lonely experience. If you don't mind having other people around, or need someone to split the rent, a roommate is the option for you. And before you go thinking, "But I need my me space!" consider this: with a good roommate, you'll always have someone to hang out with, you won't have to worry about going to social events Han style,[53] and you won't have to worry about having a heart attack and dying in the living room, leaving the neighbors to find your sun-bleached bones a week later after they've been picked clean by a band of possums who have found their way into the house.

But having a roommate can be a trying experience. If you've had a rough day and want to get away from it all, you're not as likely to be pleased to see your roomie plopped down on your couch watching your TV and eating your Cheetos. In fact, you may explode into a rage and beat him/her with household objects. When the police are dragging you away in cuffs for bludgeoning your roommate with a toaster, you'll be lamenting the fact that no one was there to give you some tips on proper roommate etiquette. Well, put down that toaster and listen up, because here they are!

Tips for Proper Roommate Etiquette

1. KNOW WHAT YOU'RE IN FOR: FRIEND VS. ACQUAINTANCE VS. STRANGER.

Being roommates with your friends may seem like the ultimate living arrangement: the two of you are buds, after all, so you'll know exactly what you're in for. WRONG. Living with someone is very different than hanging out with them sporadically. When you live with someone, it's much harder to get a reprieve from any of their habits that may annoy you, like their inability to apologize or their tendency to play dubstep all the friggin' time. With someone you don't know as well, you'll probably feel more open to discussing these annoying habits with them since you don't have anything to lose. But with an established pal, you've got a friendship on the line, which is an element that will frequently cause people to clam up about what's bothering them only to have it come gushing out like a bitter volcano. All in all it's often easier to room with someone you don't know as well, which is part of why dorm rooms are randomly assigned. If you're not living in a dorm and decide to go the full Monty and get a complete stranger as a

---

[53] Solo.

roommate, check up on them a bit first. Meet them a couple of times before you offer them copies of your house keys and things like that. If you get a bad vibe off of them, tell them you've already filled the vacancy in your living space. Better to pay a little extra rent for a while than accidentally room with a nutjob.

2. SET GROUND RULES. Human beings are often surprisingly adept at following rules. It's a peculiar trait we've evolved as time has gone on, helping us to keep order and generally behave like something other than wild animals. When you and your roommate first move in together, have an open discussion about the kinds of rules you want to set. If you need a few hours of quiet time each night or don't want them smoking inside, let them know. Living together is a two-way street, y'know.

3. COMMUNICATE OPENLY AND POLITELY. If something is bothering you, let your roommate know. They're not psychic. Or at least they're probably not psychic because if they were, they'd be so rich, they wouldn't need to split the rent with someone.

4. PETS SHOULDN'T BE ADOPTED LIGHTLY. Pets can seriously change the tenuous balance of a living situation. Often they will alter what had been a fairly harmonious living situation into one filled with the smell of poop and the sound of scrabbling claws and yowling animals. Unless it's something small and quiet like a goldfish or an African Fuzzy Rock,[54] you need to realize that having a pet will affect everyone you live with no matter how conscientious you are about it.

5. AGREE ON A ZOMBIE EVACUATION PLAN. If you plan on waiting out the zombie apocalypse in a pawn shop, let your roommate know so he doesn't plan to hightail it out to the country to avoid the thickest crowds of undead. If neither of you can agree on a survival plan, purchase walkie talkies so you can keep in contact while the zombie hordes ravage what remains of civilization.

6. DON'T DRAG OTHER PEOPLE INTO DISPUTES. If you get in a dispute with your roomie, which odds are you eventually will, keep it between the two of you. Don't drag your other friends into it and for God's sake, don't drag your other roommates into it. If you're living with multiple people, the last thing you want is everyone splitting up and taking sides, leaving your home feeling like two rival countries demarcated by a demilitarized zone in the center.

7. BE WILLING TO COMPROMISE. People who accept compromise are more likely to be

---

[54] African Fuzzy Rocks don't eat or sleep, and are like regular rocks in every way except for the lustrous mop of hair they have across their tops.

successful in virtually every aspect of their lives. Marriage, work, school, all of these require compromise, and your relationship with your roommate is no different. If you have a dispute, be it minor or major, try to find a way to meet them in the middle.

8. DISCUSS BIG CHANGES BEFORE THEY HAPPEN. If you plan on moving out, or you're

DISPUTE	COMPROMISE
Roomie doesn't do dishes.	Agree to do dishes if they'll vacuum/sweep.
Each of you has a TV show you want to watch at the same time.	Figure out who is at greatest risk for spoilers; whoever is at lesser risk can either wait or watch it online.
Your roomie is a werewolf, and you are a vampire.	Agree to keep an eye on him during full moons in exchange for him helping curb your bloodlust whenever guests show up and start exposing their necks.

sick of your roommate and want them gone, talk about it first. It can be stressful to be left in a lurch when someone spontaneously decides they're going to leave and take their half of the rent with them, so don't do that to your roommate and don't let them do that to you.

9. AGREE ON SURVIVAL SCENARIOS AHEAD OF TIME SO THINGS DON'T GET WEIRD WHEN IT'S TWENTY BELOW AND YOU'RE BOTH DYING SO YOU TRY TO SLICE YOUR ROOMMATE OPEN LIKE A TAUNTAUN AND SLIDE INSIDE FOR WARMTH. Few things are more awkward then getting ready to make a human tent out of someone, only to find out they had other ideas.[55]

Once you get to know your roommates, it can often become much easier to live with them. They know your quirks, you know theirs, and life can achieve a harmonious balance. Oddly enough, after spending enough time with your co-habitaters, you may find they're different than you initially thought. Some of them might be lazier at home than they are in the outside world, or maybe they're more reclusive and paranoid than you've come to believe. It's these sorts of quirks that led the top anthropologists of the geek world to categorize roommates into several distinct categories.

---

[55] It's why I had to kick out my last roommate. Anytime the temperature outside got below 40, he'd grab a lightsaber and start dropping hints about how chilly he was.

The Seven Types of Geek Roommates

THE JABBA. The Jabba rarely, if ever, leaves your living space. He just sits on the couch all day long, content to watch *Farscape* on Netflix and chow down on Fritos. Messes are a high problem with Jabbas, as are smells, and it'll take more than a polite reminder or two to get him to clean up after himself. If all else fails, try a cattle prod.

THE COLLECTOR. We geeks have a tendency to nest. We want to collect things and show them off so the world can see just how awesome we are. The Collector takes this to a new level, with his posters, boxed action figures, and anime wall scrolls spilling out of his room and into the other areas of the house like some sort of multi-colored sci-fi fungus. Collectors tend to be good about following the rules and react well to being told to remove their stuff. Like a plant they need pruning, as no matter how many times you cut down their things, you'll still have to remove an errant wall scroll or two every few months.

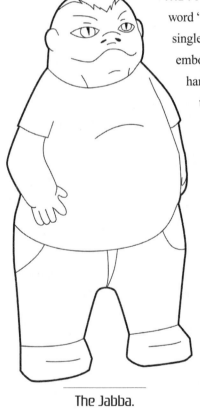

The Jabba.

THE TV ZEALOT. "Fan" is a term that stems from the word "fanatical," meaning filled with obsessive and single-minded zeal, and the TV Zealot is the absolute embodiment of this ideal. The Zealot has a show (or handful of shows) she *must* see at their *proper* airing time or she won't know what anyone's talking about the next day and someone might end up spoiling the big end-of-episode twist. All must be silent when their show is on or face the wrath of a TV remote being hurled at their head. Though you might suggest to the TV Zealot that she simply take to the internet to watch her shows, she will often refuse out of fear of reading spoilers on Facebook or Twitter.

THE TECH JUNKIE. The room of a Tech Junkie looks like someone put a stick of dynamite inside of a terminator and blew it up, leaving its metal innards on every flat surface with room to hold them. He'll run your power bill through the roof, and will often heat up the entire house with the radiation coming from his nuclear computer

The Neo.

The TV Guide Zealot.

rig, but he'll know the answer to virtually every tech problem you could ever have and will gladly help you upgrade your computer when the time comes.

THE PARENT. Perhaps they had to grow up too fast or perhaps they're just missing their own parents after moving away from home, but some geek roommates will, upon flying out of the nest, transform into younger versions of their parents. Maybe they enjoy cooking all the time, or spend half of their free time cleaning, or perhaps they like to pay for everything and insist you follow a strict set of ground rules lest you be spanked. Having the Parent as a roommate is a double-edged sword, and be warned that they can revert at any moment back into their Young Adult selves, leaving you hungry and poor when they're not cooking you hot meals and funding your Lego addiction.

THE NEO. You know a bit about computers, sure, but not as much as the Neo. At least, not as much as the Neo says he does. He's constantly clacking away at his keyboard, his screen filled with DOS prompts and his speakers filled with techno. He likes to think he's the most dangerous man in America, when really the greatest bit of "hacking" he's ever done is when he guessed the password to his English teacher's email.

THE BATMAN. Also known as the Ultimate Roommate, the Batman is gone most of the time, with a room that is as pristine as it is unlived-in. He always pays his half of the bills, though, and never makes a mess. It's the ultimate living situation, except, of course, for the small chance that your roommate is the *real* Batman, in which case you may find yourself kidnapped by one of his supervillain arch-rivals. If you suspect your roommate is actually Batman, don't dig around his stuff to try to find the truth. If you're right, then the guy's gone through enough already, what with his parents getting shot and everything.

Pets, Our Fuzzy Freeloaders

If you prefer your companionship to be of the four-legged kind (and aren't into any kind of weird human horse-riding S & M) then you may want to get a pet. Pets are fun, cute, and on the average. people who have pets live longer.[56] They aren't perfect, though. Their costs can vary widely depending on what kind of pet you get, how sickly they are and how inclined they are toward tearing up your couch. And most pets are *highly* amoral. They'll wreck your screen door and not even say a word about it, or throw up in your shoes without having the decency to give you a heads-up before you slide your feet in. Yes, your furry friends will sometimes annoy you, but they have the all-powerful ability to get you to forgive them thanks to their utter cuteness. Some pets are cuter than others, however, so if your pug errs a little more on the side of pugly than cute, consider dressing him up in a costume.

COSTUME: THE WAMPUG

SOURCE MATERIAL: *THE EMPIRE STRIKES BACK*

CUTENESS: 10

EASILY PURCHASED? NO

EASILY CONSTRUCTED? YES

To construct a Wampug costume, first locate a pug, and then wrap him in fake white fur. Tie it all together with string and throw a couple of plush horns on his head for added Wamposity.

COSTUME: DOGIMUS PRIME

SOURCE MATERIAL: *TRANSFORMERS*

CUTENESS: 10

EASILY PURCHASED? YES

EASILY CONSTRUCTED? YES

Given the plethora of *Transformers* kids costumes available, constructing an Optimus Prime outfit for your pet should be no problem. For the movie Optimus Prime, shorten the arms and legs on the kid's costume and then dress your pet in it. For Original, a.k.a Generation One Optimus Prime, locate several cardboard boxes both small and large. Paint most of the larger boxes red and two of them blue. Place the blue boxes on your pet's back feet and the red boxes on its chest/forelegs. For the face, either print up a picture of Optimus Prime's face and use it as a mask or construct your own out of cardboard. If you own two or more pets, try constructing more transformers and creating an entire fleet of Autobots and Decepticons.

---

[56] Except, of course, for the nutcases who decide that dogs are just too *passe* and instead opt for a pet mountain lion, which promptly tears its owner's face off.

COSTUME: SUPERDOG

SOURCE MATERIAL: *ACTION COMICS* #1 (FIRST APPEARANCE OF SUPERMAN)

CUTENESS: 10

EASILY PURCHASED? YES

EASILY CONSTRUCTED? YES

Buy a red towel. Tie it around your dog's neck. Congratulations, you've created a Superdog. For added realism, load your dog into a rocket and shoot it into space, then blow up your dog's home planet.

COSTUME: KHAL DOGGO

SOURCE MATERIAL: *GAME OF THRONES*

CUTENESS: 10

EASILY PURCHASED? NO

EASILY CONSTRUCTED? NO

Let me get this out of the way: dogs don't like wearing eyeshadow. Maybe it's because they think they're cute without makeup, or maybe they don't like not being able to touch their face for fear of smearing it, but whatever the reason, your dog will not like having on makeup, nor is it likely to enjoy wearing a long braided wig. But when you see that proud beast prancing into the room, covered in leather armor and looking like the greatest warrior in the land, your heart will swell with pride and you'll forget all the time you spent smearing makeup on your dog.

COSTUME: BATCAT

SOURCE MATERIAL: *DETECTIVE COMICS* #1 (FIRST APPEARANCE OF BATMAN)

CUTENESS: 10

EASILY PURCHASED? YES

EASILY CONSTRUCTED? YES

Criminals *beware!* There's a friggin' cat dressed like Batman running around and it's looking for a little night-time justice. For a Batcat costume, all you really need is some kind of Batman mask and a black cape, both of which can be found in any costume store or toy aisle.

COSTUME: SAURON

SOURCE MATERIAL: *THE LORD OF THE RINGS*

Clockwise from top left: Superdog, Dogimus Prime, The Wampug, Khal Doggo.

CUTENESS: 10

EASILY PURCHASED? NO

EASILY CONSTRUCTED? NO

Learning metalworking is a tricky thing, but it's a lot trickier to explain to your local blacksmith that you want him to forge a set of spiked metal armor so your cat can look like Sauron. I *suppose* you could just paint some cardboard again, but, when it comes to dressing up as the true master of the One Ring, I'd suggest doing it right so he doesn't notice your shortcuts and get mad about it. And he will notice. He's a giant floating eye; all he does all day is sit around and Peeping Tom people.

COSTUME: MARIO

SOURCE MATERIAL: *SUPER MARIO BROS*

CUTENESS: 10

EASILY PURCHASED? YES

EASILY CONSTRUCTED? YES

Buy your pet a red hat. Voila, you have Mario. You can add a red shirt and overalls if you'd like, but as long as you have the hat, your point will be made. If you have more than one pet, buy a green hat so one can be Mario and the other can be Luigi. Swap hats once in a while, so neither pet grows to resent the other for getting to play Mario all the time.

COSTUME: ZORDOG

SOURCE MATERIAL: *MIGHTY MORPHIN' POWER RANGERS*

CUTENESS: 10

EASILY PURCHASED? CANNOT BE PURCHASED

EASILY CONSTRUCTED? HEAVENS NO

Your first step is to get a PhD in theoretical physics. Once you've mastered all the intangible elements of the universe, convert your dog into a being of pure energy and store him in a tube. Continue taking him for walks (put the tube in a wagon if you have to) and face the tube toward the windows so your dog can still bark at the outside world. Only keep him like that for pictures or for the Halloween season, however, or else your Zordog will start attracting all sorts of monsters, worrisome robots and teenagers with attitudes.

Cleanliness: It's the Latest Thing!

Cleaning your home may seem like an alien concept to some, but it's the latest craze

Clockwise from top left: Batcat, Mario, Mega Cat, Sauron.

that's really *sweeping* the nation. Keeping a clean home helps people feel more energized, less depressed, and helps fight off disease and allergies, so if you want to keep healthy and keep your guests happy, here are a few pointers on cleaning up:

- Clean out your leftovers once in a while. If you open a container and the food cries out to you, kill it with fire and discard.
- If your dishes smell bad, put them in the dishwasher. If you don't have a dishwasher, wash them by hand. If you don't have hands, lick them clean or pay someone to lick them for you.
- Spot cleaning big messes is much easier than trying to scrub them out later on, after they've had a chance to dry up and harden. Stains are like RPG characters—much easier to kill when they're level one and haven't had a chance to level up and grow stronger. The longer you leave old spaghetti sauce on the carpet, the more it'll level up. Leave it too long and it may learn magic, magic it will use to destroy *you* with.
- Disinfectants aren't just for hospitals. Cleaning your tables and counters with disinfectants helps destroy bacteria around the house and helps you not get sick as often.
- Dust and clean your controllers and keyboards once in a while. Ernest Weebler, a well-known writer from the early '80s, lived and died by his keyboard. Literally. Turns out he'd eaten one too many meals at his keyboard and the moldy contents within it evolved into a complex life form that sprung forth and attacked him, choking him to death in a matter of seconds. It took the combined might of Kurt Russell and Sylvester Stallone to take the thing out, and the harrowing experience became the inspiration for both Russell's *The Thing* and Stallone's *Stop or My Mom Will Shoot*.
- Vacuum your carpet and sweep your floors.
- If you have a baby, consider getting a babymop to let your little tyke clean up while he/she crawls around.

How to Manage Your Hard-Earned Space Bucks: Geeking Out on a Budget

Managing money can be tough for anyone, especially geeks. After all, we have so many awesome hobbies and toys that we want to buy that it could leave us wondering how on Earth we're going to afford it all. Economizing, my dear, economizing. If most adults want to afford things, they have to budget their money carefully, something that most geeks won't have a problem with, seeing as how they probably earn more money than most people and are smarter i.e. better at math. Let's look at an example geek budget to see how it's done:

- **MONTHLY EARNINGS:** $800
- **RENT (SPLIT WITH TWO OTHER ROOMMATES):** $270/month
- **UTILITIES:** $60/month
- **FOOD:** $200/month
- **GAS:** $60/month

That's $590 a month, which leaves $210 for other things. Now, it's never a good idea to spend every cent you have in a given month. If you've got the money to spare, you should save some in case of an emergency or in case there's a really sweet deal on iPads. It's often recommended you save at least 10 percent of your income, which in this hypothetical case would be $80 but it would probably be safer to round up to an even $100. Now that you've got $110 dollars of disposable income, let's look at the types of geeky things you may want to purchase:

TIME-SENSITIVE: Video games, movie tickets, books.

In an age where spoilers are virtually inescapable thanks to social media, it's important to stay ahead of, or at least even with, the curve on anything that could potentially be spoiled for you. Likewise, with the amount of multiplayer found in most games, it's best to purchase them when they first come out. Waiting to buy can sometimes mean you're playing a two-month-old game when everyone else has already moved on to the next one.

TIME/COST VARIABLE: Collectibles.

Collectibles are something that can generally wait to be purchased when you have more money *except* for the instances where there's an exceptional deal going on. For example, if you see a limited edition Master Chief figurine on sale for 3 percent off, you can probably wait to buy it. However, if some fool is selling *X-Men* #1 for $15 bucks on eBay, I'd say it's safe to throw down the cash necessary to buy it.

Now, as much as you might be tempted to, you don't *have* to spend all of your money on yourself like a selfish bastard. If you're so inclined, there are a number of causes worthy of devoting your cash to, special causes any geek can feel good about donating to.

chapter twelve

with great

geekdom

comes great responsibility: doing good as a geek

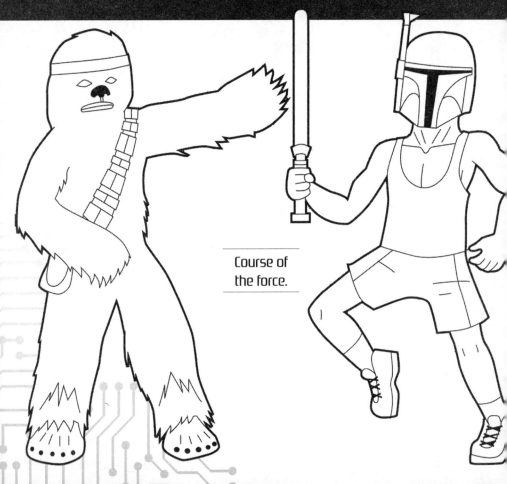

Course of the force.

> "Is the rich world aware of how four billion of the six billion live? If we were aware, we would want to help out, we'd want to get involved."
> — Bill Gates, co-founder of Microsoft and philanthropist

Now that you've established yourself a bit—having acquired some friends, gotten a job, and earned yourself a place to call home—perhaps it's time you thought about giving back to your community. Generally when people give to charity, they like to find a cause that inspires them personally. You'll see animal lovers giving to the ASPCA, cancer survivors donating to cancer research, and people who own feral goochcats giving to the Feral Goochcats Awareness Fund.[57] And as a geek, you've got plenty of options for geeky charities worthy of your time and donations.

Course of the Force

Course of the Force is much like a normal relay race, only instead of standard batons, the runners pass lightsabers from one to another. The event was put together in order to benefit the Make-A-Wish foundation, a quality charity focused on trying to grant the wishes of extremely sick kids.

---

[57] If you don't know what a goochcat is, don't ask. They hate that.

Child's Play

Founded in 2003 by Jerry "Penny Arcade" Holkins and Mike "Don't Call Me Gabe" Krahulik, Child's Play is an organization dedicated to helping sick children through the donation of toys and video games. Let's face it—being in a hospital can be a boring, often scary experience, especially for kids. Thanks to Child's Play, there are countless hospitals now equipped with playthings for kids to help them pass the time. They have a wish list set up through Amazon.com to let donors purchase the items directly and have them sent where they're needed. Some other, less reputable charities have grown notorious for accepting monetary donations in the name of some important cause only to turn around and spend 75 percent or more of the funds on themselves and "spreading awareness" instead of, y'know, actually doing some good with it. By purchasing these items directly, you can be certain your money is actually going toward what it's supposed to.

In addition to monetary donations, you can also give away your old playthings, so if you've got an old GameCube you're not using, you can pop on over to Childsplaycharity.org and find out how you can get it set up in a local children's hospital or pediatric ward. The only thing I'll add is that if you're thinking of donating something crappy, like *Big Rigs: Over the Road Racing* or *Superman 64*, don't. These kids have enough crap to deal with already.

We Can Be Heroes

DC Comics launched this charity in order to help combat starvation in Africa. In order to help spread awareness of their charity, they're using Batman, Wonder Woman, Superman, and many of their other iconic characters to get the message out. DC Comics has also vowed to make its financial records 100 percent available to the public in order to make it clear that they are not organizing this as an easy cash-grab.

Clash of the Geeks

Authored by such legends as Wil Wheaton, John Scalzi, Catherynne M. Valente, Stephen Toulouse and more, *Clash of the Geeks* is a fun-filled e-book that was put together to help benefit the Lupus Alliance of America. The book contains a variety of short-form literature, including short stories, poems, and, oddly enough, at least one musical number.

Donors Choose

According to the Donors Choose website, the charity is organized in the style of a wish list: teachers and other educators post request for school supplies their classrooms need, such as pencils, microscopes, new books, etc., and people pay for the individual requests. It's as simple as that.

Wikipedia

I know, donating to Wikipedia feels like a strange idea. After all, it's *Wikipedia*. Why would it need money? I'll tell you why: because the folks behind Wikipedia believe that, like a public park or library, their website is no place for advertisements. And being the fifth most used website on the internet (behind things like Facebook, Google, and Catswearingspats.com) requires a lot of bandwidth, which, in turn, requires a lot of money. Donating to Wikipedia is much like donating to PBS—you're helping invest money into something because the people behind it are just looking to educate and enlighten, not get rich. If people stopped donating to Wikipedia, it'd probably have to devolve into some Geocities-esque pop-up-ad-laden nightmare, filled with flashing gifs and garish colors.

Creative Commons

Creative Commons is an organization dedicated to helping creative-type people pay for and deal with boring, legal, and technical mumbo-jumbo which impedes the creative process and drags everyone down. The stuff they do is boring, but it helps out the people who make the things we all love, like webseries, Youtube channels, and Frodo X Legolas slash fiction.

Fund Science

It's an unfortunate state of affairs in modern society when things like *Jersey Shore* receive more funding than SETI.[58] It's a crying shame, and one that you, personally, can help rectify. Fund Science presents charitable souls with the opportunity to look through and donate to different scientific projects they believe to be worthwhile. Some of the projects are grounded, things such as water purification systems for third-world countries, and others are a little more out there, like a physics engine designed to punch a hole in space and time and let alternate realities come pouring in.[59]

---

[58] The Search for Extra-Terrestrial Intelligence. They're the guys out there trying to find E.T. so we can give him a hug, or trying to give everyone a little bit of warning when the Reapers descend on Earth.
[59] I'm not one to tell you how to spend your money, but, if given the choice, I'd recommend you don't donate money to that last one. It sounds like a freakin' doomsday device.

chapter thirteen

cooking

Using Your Bat'leth to Prepare Thanksgiving Dinner

Cooking with Worf.

"This is my invariable advice to people: Learn how to cook—try new recipes, learn from your mistakes, be fearless, and above all have fun!"
— Julia Child, chef, author, and one of the world's first food geeks

F ood. We all need it unless we're aliens, zombies, robots, or some kind of alien zombie robot. For those who aren't ali-zom-bots, you have two options: purchase fast food for every meal of your life, which would get costly quick, not to mention the toll on your health, if the *Super Size Me* guy is to be believed, or you can learn to cook for yourself.

Food preparation can seem daunting for those of us more inclined toward keyboards and touch screens than cutting boards and cheese graters, but it doesn't have to be. We geeks are a powerful niche, and every industry from food to fashion wants a piece of our bank account. If you're looking for some vittles with a geeky flair and aren't ready to hit the kitchen yet, there's always old standbys like Mountain Dew or Doritos. But if you're looking for a bit more sustenance, you'll have to slay the fire-breathing beast known as "The Uh-venn."

Fighting Back Your Dark Hunger: Cooking It Old School

Before we get started in the kitchen, there are a few basic tools you'll need to familiarize yourself with. For non-food geeks, try to think of these tools as your weapon, and the meal as a monster in need of slaying. Like any monster, you need a specialized set of weapons to really hone in on its weak points and bring it down, such as:

- **SILVERWARE:** forks, spoons and knives. Okay, even the most food-tarded among us knows what silverware is, right? Good, everyone does so we can move on ... wait, no. I see a young man with a cowlick raising his hand. He doesn't know what silverware is. *Fine.* Just know that the spoon is the round one, the fork is the pokey one, and the knife is the cutty one.

- **MEASURING CUPS.** As their name implies, measuring cups are used to measure out specific amounts of ingredients. If you're familiar with the metric system, then you should have no problem increasing or decreasing the amount of required ingredients based on the amount of food you're preparing. If you're lucky enough to live in a non-metric country like the U.S. or Narnia, then you'll need to figure out how many of X are in Y. Here's a conversion chart to help with this confusing matter.

1 liquid gallon = 4 quarts	1 liquid quart = 2 pints
1 liquid pint = 2 cups	1 liquid cup = 7 quimlets
1 quimlet= 8.2 tonkles	1 tonkle= 1 liquid gallon

- **CUTTING BOARDS.** When cooking, you will occasionally have to cut things up and it is important to do so without destroying your countertops. Cutting boards are sturdy, flat pieces of plastic or wood that are used to slice and dice whatever foods your little heart desires. Be careful while dicing, as it's common amongst nubile cooks for them to get overexcited at the prospect of dicing up cucumbers and they end up taking off a finger or two.

- **MIXING BOWLS.** Most baked goods and necromantic rituals make good use of a mixing bowl, which is a thick bowl used to blend flour, sugar, and/or human blood, depending on the recipe and your level of necromantic prowess.

- Pots and pans. Pots are for cooking soup and pans are for searing meat except for the times when they're not.

> "I like my blood wine very young and very sweet."
> — Lt. Worf, *Star Trek: The Next Generation*

- **BAKING TRAYS.** Baking trays are used to bake. Since they get to make fun things like cakes and brownies, they're often the favorite around the kitchen, which can lead to jealousy and unrest from your other kitchen utensils. Keep an eye on your mixing bowls so they don't try to bump off the baking trays in a heavy-handed attempt to become number one.

- **WEIRD LITTLE METAL THINGS WITH DOODADS ON THE END.** I'll be honest here—somewhere along the line, people started including these doodads in every kitchen set even though no one knows what they do. There's one with a spiral thing at the end, one shaped like a 2D lightbulb, one with a Cthulhu face on it ... the list is endless. Just throw them all in a drawer and let them pile up until the thing jams shut. If the drawer has become so overcrowded you can't open it anymore, mission accomplished.

- **KNOW YOUR KNIVES:** Certain types of knives are specialized to certain types of material. Serrated knives (the knives with the little rough edges on the blade) are good for cutting through tough materials like meat or cement blocks. Flat knives are good for vegetables and cheese, and silver knives are good for werewolves and vampires.

- **KNOW YOUR SPICES:** Spices come in three basic types: salt, pepper, and other. Put some salt and pepper on everything you cook, add other at your own discretion.

- **KNOW YOUR RS:** Ranch, Ramen and Ravioli. It's a common fact that ranch is the most powerful of all dressings. It overpowers the flavor of almost anything it's applied to, putting a chokehold on dull, healthy foods like salads and carrots until they cry uncle and give in to its ranch-y goodness. It's for this reason that many use it as flavoring for almost anything, like french fries, pizza, and ice cream.

Ramen noodles are the cheapest meal a person can eat without resorting to something drastic like frying up bugs using an exposed power line. Ramen comes in a variety of flavors, and can be eaten cooked or raw.[60]

---

[60] Most people think eating raw ramen is yucky. I agree. But still, to each his own. In junior high I knew a guy who liked to eat his cafeteria tray, which just goes to show you that good taste is relative.

Now that you've been introduced to the most common kitchen implements, hopefully shaking hands with them and making polite conversation along the way, it's time to move on to advanced kitchening: recipes. Recipes are the blueprints to make the food you want, and only you have the power to make them. Are you a bad enough dude to cook crème brûlée?

Recipes: You've Gotta Do the Cooking By the Book

SUBMARINER SANDWICH

- **RECIPE LEVEL:** Basic

  Get a loaf of French bread, cut it open, and add deli meat, cheese, and vegetables to your liking. Once you've constructed the sandwich, have it hit on the Invisible Woman incessantly and then fade into obscurity.

TARDIP

- **RECIPE LEVEL:** Basic

  Melt a bowl of Velveeta or similarly creamy cheese in the microwave. Stir occasionally and add in spices, tomatoes, green chilies, and milk for flavor and texture. Upon the dip's completion, send it on a journey through time and space.

JABBA WAFFLES

- **RECIPE LEVEL:** Basic

  Buy frozen waffles. Toast them. Add green food coloring.

JABBA FLAKES

- **RECIPE LEVEL:** Basic

  Buy Corn Flakes. Add green food coloring.

JABBA CHILI

- **RECIPE LEVEL:** Basic

  Make Chili. Add green food coloring. Throw away because it now looks disgusting. Order pizza instead.

NATHAN DRAKE'S THIEVIN' BARBECUE BURGER

- **RECIPE LEVEL:** Basic

  Wait until your friend is eating a barbecue burger. Steal it from him. Spout one-liners as you escape, climbing onto a nearby rooftop as you eat your purloined meal.

FRIED CHEETO DUST BALL

- **RECIPE LEVEL:** Intermediate

  Shake your keyboard into a bowl. Take dusty keyboard contents and mold them into a sphere. Deep fry your Cheeto ball using whatever oil you think tastes best. (Motor oil is not recommended). Garnish and serve with Mountain Dew. Eat meal at computer. Repeat process.

HUNGER GAMES HUNGRY MAN NACHOS

- **RECIPE LEVEL:** Advanced

  Brown beef or thoroughly cook chicken breast. Add taco seasoning and chilies for flavor. When the meat is finished, dice it up finely. Place atop of chips and add in beans, salsa, sour cream, guacamole, and cheese. Eat while watching people fight to the death for your own amusement.

"I know what I need! I need ... I need ... I need ... fish fingers and custard!"
— Dr. Who, *The Eleventh Hour*

A Fried Cheeto Dust Ball can be yours in three easy steps.

STEP 1

STEP 2

STEP 3

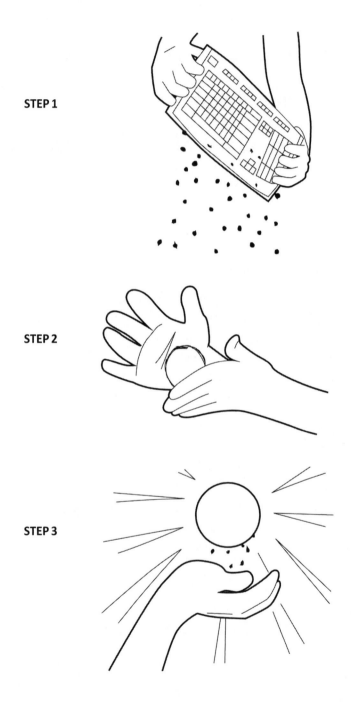

Nutrition: Get You Some!

Eating a proper diet can feel like a hassle. How much Vitamin C do you need everyday? Is fiber good for you? If I eat after midnight will I turn into a gremlin?[61] To help relieve any confusion you might have, I've assembled a few pointers on how to eat healthy.

- Buy a pack of vitamins and try to eat one everyday. Some of the adult ones can be a bit on the chalky side, so it may be easier to eat them if you get kids vitamins. And remember that these vitamins are there to supplement the healthy foods you should be eating, not replacing them. Just because you're popping Fred Flintstone in your mouth doesn't mean you can stop eating salad.
- Eat fruits and vegetables. Lots of them. NOW!
- Cake does not constitute a food group, no matter how much we all wish it did.
- If you're looking to cut down on your calories, there's two easy steps you can take:
    - 1. Count the calories of all the food you're eating.
    - 2. Brush your teeth often. You're not likely to want to eat when your mouth is minty clean.
- Fruit is better for you than fruit juice. An apple has way more vitamins and fiber than a glass of apple juice, and generally a lot less sugar, so try to eat the real thing if it's available.
- Carbs can be good for you. Carbohydrates are the lovable rogue of the nutrition world—good one second, bad the next, and all along they secretly have a heart of gold. While yes, carbs can be high calorie, they also help you feel full longer, so it's a bad idea to cut them out of your diet entirely, as it will lead to inevitable snacking.
- Some "healthy" foods can be surprisingly high-calorie or surprisingly low in nutritional value. Read the label before buying any new health foods.

---

[61] Lots. No. Probably not.

chapter fourteen

boldly go

where lots of people have gone before
the best places for geeks to visit

> "Remember what Bilbo used to say: 'It's a dangerous business, Frodo, going out your door. You step onto the road, and if you don't keep your feet, there's no knowing where you might be swept off to.' "
> — J.R.R. Tolkien, *The Lord of the Rings*

After months of putting in eight hours a day at the ol' salt mine,[62] you need to blow off some steam. Enter: the vacation. Sure you could visit the Grand Canyon and be wowed at its natural wonders, or head to NYC and get in touch with how much you love *AMERICA*. But if you're looking to relax with a trip that's a little more catered to we-who-are-pale-of-skin-and-big-of-brain, then a regular vacation is out of the question. It's time to take a geekcation. Geekcations are much like regular vacations, but with a higher chance of zombies. When considering your options on where to go, think about visiting some of these fine locales that have been enjoyed by your fellow geeks.

---

[62] I hope you don't work at a salt mine. If you do, quit. It sounds dangerous there, what with all the cave-ins and salt monsters running around.

Top Five Geeky Vacation Spots

ROSWELL, NEW MEXICO. Roswell. Aliens. Aliens. Roswell. The two have practically become synonyms in American culture. Those of us who want to keep our eyes on the stars and believe that the truth is out there will likely enjoy a vacation to America's most famous purported alien crash site. If Hollywood movies are accurate, and why wouldn't they be, then you'll have a small chance of seeing real aliens while visiting Roswell, as well as getting caught up in the ensuing government conspiracy. When this happens, you should keep calm, stretch before running, and upload all of your pictures to your Facebook in case the government mind-washes you to erase your memory.

NEW ZEALAND. *The Lord of the Rings* movies were filmed across a substantial part of New Zealand. While it's unlikely you'll be able to find the One Ring and join your own Fellowship of the Ring, you can, at the very least, walk where Frodo walked and get attacked by trees where those orcs got attacked by trees.

LOS ANGELES, CA. Since a majority of Hollywood films are made, well, near Hollywood, visiting Los Angeles means you're likely to see some of the famous locales of your favorite movies. The caves from *Pirates of the Caribbean*, the eagles and vultures from *Birdemic 2: The Resurrection*—they're all there! Sure, they might look a little cooler in the movies, and sure, some parts of L.A. are so filthy and inhospitable they border on post-apocalyptic, but who cares when you're standing at the same spot your favorite movie heroes did years before!

WILLY WONKA'S CHOCOLATE FACTORY. Sure, the tickets are hard to come by, but if you're pure of heart and have a few bucks to spare on a Wonka bar, you might be able to score a tour of the elusive Willy Wonka's chocolate factory. I've never been myself, but rumor has it that it's filled with amazing sights such as chocolate rivers, Oompaloompas, and fat German kids stuck in pipes.

CONVENTIONS. Conventions are the ultimate geek vacation. Like most geeks themselves, conventions come in a variety of shapes and sizes, all offering different flavors of excitement for you to sample. Which vacation is right for you is all a matter of your interests, which is why I've broken down a few of the most popular cons based on their topics.

Home is Where the Hulk is:
Top Five Conventions Geeks Must Attend

THE ELECTRONIC ENTERTAINMENT EXPO, LOS ANGELES, CA. E3 is a convention highlighting the amazing new games you'll see on the shelves soon. Though it used to be open to the public, E3 has shifted toward being a more journalist-oriented show, but, if you've maintained any kind of a geeky blog, you've got a good shot at getting a pass to attend. You've also got to be 17 or older to go, partly because of the aforementioned journalistic requirement and also because they occasionally show off a game which features nipples or decapitations.

THE PENNY ARCADE EXPO, SEATTLE, WA, AND BOSTON, MA. PAX was created by the masterminds behind *Penny Arcade*, Mike Krahulik and Jerry Holkins, as a celebration of gamer culture. Thanks to E3 shutting its doors to the public, PAX has become something of a hotspot for game companies to show off their newest games to the eager fans and for those eager fans to come together to compete, connect, and just generally hang out.

GEN CON, INDIANAPOLIS, IN. Those with a flair for fantasy and tabletop gaming may find themselves attracted to Gen Con. And I'm not talking a schoolgirl crush—Gen Con's stuffed to the brim with *Magic the Gathering*, *Dungeons and Dragons*, and every other type of tabletop gaming goodness you could desire. No, I'm talking full on, want to kiss them on the mouth, and feel them up under the bleachers kind of attraction.[63] Gen Con also has plenty to offer the avid LARPer, like an amazing life-sized dungeon crawl. Before you buy your tickets and get your +5 foam vorpal blade all shined up and ready to go, be warned that those attending are often so zealous about their costumes and role-playing games that they forget to do things such as bathe and brush their teeth. It's become enough of a problem that the Gen Con pamphlets often cover basic hygiene to help keep the B.O. levels to a sufferable level.

CONSUMER ELECTRONICS SHOW, LAS VEGAS, NV. You know that scene in every classic James Bond movie where Q shows Bond his incredible new gadgets that won't be on the market for the next ten years? CES is like that, only it's massive and everything you see will be on sale soon. Groundbreaking technology is often first unveiled at CES. Nothing major, only little things like VCRs, the Nintendo, and 3DTVs. It's rumored that 2015 will unveil the first personal assistant robot, PEAR. There aren't any Consumer Electronic

---

[63] If you do want to feel up Gencon under the bleachers, try to be subtle about it.

Shows scheduled for 2016 or beyond due to the rebellion of the PEARs and the extinction of the human race at the hands of these politely murderous androids.

SAN DIEGO COMIC-CON, SAN DIEGO, CA. SDCC could be considered the ultimate geek convention. Attended by over 150,000 people every year, this convention has exploded from the small, comics-oriented con it was in 1970 into a mammoth celebration of all things nerdy. There's comics, movies, video games, TV shows—it has everything! SDCC has so many things, in fact, that much of it will leave you wondering why the hell it's at a geek convention, like panels for *Twilight* and *Ally Mcbeal*.[64] It's a hectic convention, and people have gotten stabbed over seating,[65] so if you plan to attend such a gigantic convention, you'll need to get prepared for what lies in store for you. Even if you've attended other cons, you will not be ready for SDCC. It is a monstrous beast unto itself, one hungry for ill-prepared geeks, but totally worth the risk.

The Handy Convention Survival Guide

- **FRIEND/FOLLOW NEW PALS QUICKLY.** When you get a group of geeks together, we like to throw a *lot* of nerdy-ass parties, filled with highbrow jokes and obscure references. If you attend any of these shindigs, you're likely to meet a lot of new people, so many that it can be hard to keep track of them. While friending someone on Facebook might be a little more personal than you care for, following them on Twitter shouldn't be. And if you're reading this in some kind of strange future that lacks any form of Twitter or Facebook, then you have bigger things to worry about than social networking, like the army of PEARs closing in on your human resistance base.

- **BRING FOOD.** Convention food is expensive, the lines are long, and it's generally pretty crummy. Bring snacks to munch on while attending your con of choice and then go eat a hearty meal at the end of the day.

- **TRY TO STAY IN A CLOSE HOTEL, PREFERABLY ONE WITH A BREAKFAST BUFFET.** Getting around in a new city can be a hassle if you're unfamiliar with the rules of public transportation there. The closer you are to the actual convention, the easier

---

[64] Just kidding about the *Ally Mcbeal*, but seriously, what the hell was *Twilight* doing at SDCC?
[65] Seriously. One of the years I attended SDCC, a man was stabbed over seating for a Harry Potter panel. I guess the stabber really wanted to be in Slytherin.

Survivalist geek armed with tools for making it out of a convention alive.

your life will be. Most cons entail a lot of walking[66] and odds are you'll be pretty tired by the end of the day. Take regular breaks to rest and drink lots of water. Oh, and if your hotel has a breakfast buffet, you hit that thing with a vengeance. Eat so much food that waffles tremble when they see you coming. Not only does it help you get your money's worth from the hotel, but it will reduce the amount of overpriced convention food you'll end up eating.

- **BE COOL WHEN MEETING FAMOUS PEOPLE.** The hallmark of most any con is its special guests. While, yes, these are folks who have been involved in some amazingly special projects in their lives, you also need to remember that they're just people. Talk to them as you would any other person you're meeting, keeping fanboy/girl blubbering to a relative minimum. If you've got a story about how they've especially touched you somehow, then feel free to tell them. For example, if Levar Burton's performance as Geordi on *Star Trek: The Next Generation* inspired you to become a scientist or engineer, tell him. But if you're meeting Bruce Campbell, you may not want to steal his hair in the hopes of cloning your own personal Campbell-servant. I know he'd appreciate it.

- **FIST-BUMP, DON'T HANDSHAKE.** It's a scientific fact that the human hand has as many germs on it as a dog's anus. Shaking hands with someone is the same as sticking a finger right up a bulldog's backside, which can often lead to personal illness. Fist bump new acquaintances to help keep the spread of germs to a minimum. Feel free, however, to shake the anus of any dog you meet.

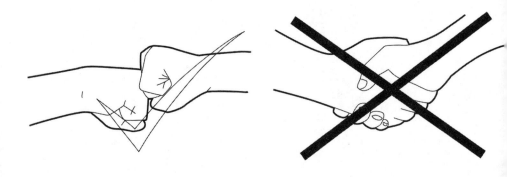

---

[66] Or, in the case of San Diego Comic-Con, a crapload of walking.

- **VISIT ARTISTS' ALLEY.**[67] Don't just chase every movie star in hopes of catching a glimpse, visit the area where artists, programmers, and other creators are drawing, signing, and talking with their fans. Especially take time to meet the older ones while you still have a chance. With comic book creators who were drawing in their teens back in World War II, it may be your last chance to meet them.
- **DON'T COUNT ON YOUR CELL PHONES.** Convention centers are notorious for killing cell phone reception, so try to stick with your group and make plans to meet up whenever you decide to break away from them.
- **FIND A SECLUDED BATHROOM.** The bathrooms at the convention center or hotel lobby are probably going to be disgusting and overcrowded, constantly covered in a thin layer of urine. Try to locate a lavatory in a secluded hallway or forgotten corner of the convention area so you can go without having to worry about accidentally stepping on a stray poo.
- **BE WARY OF LIMITED EDITIONS.** Conventions sell an endless number of "limited edition" items. Limited edition Blue Lantern Flash, limited edition Future Foundation Spider-Man, limited edition Sleepy Time Hulk Footy Pajamas with Optional Booty Flap. If you're a collector or a major fan of the characters, you should get them if that's what your heart desires. Purchasing limited edition items with plans to resell, however, will probably bite you in the butt. These items will end up rare and will sell for top dollar *when there are people willing to buy.* Unfortunately, most of the people willing to buy these kinds of things were probably at the same convention you got them at in the first place and probably have a dozen of their own sitting at home.
- **BE WARY OF DEALS TOO GOOD TO BE TRUE.** Though most shops and booths will adhere to the rules set up by the convention, organizers there are an unscrupulous few who will circumvent the system and sell wares that are less than legit. Some are fans selling illegal copies of a strange live-action Sailor Moon featuring a handicapped teen in a laser-shooting wheelchair, which, despite not quite being on the up-and-up, is still just a fan trying to sell things they like. Other times you'll get people selling knock-off DVD box sets of TV shows, with each DVD in a shoddy plastic sleeve and the name written across it in permanent marker, or

[67] The area of a convention set aside for artists to hang out, sell their things, and occasionally draw unflattering caricatures of you.

guys selling "video game collections," which are really collections of ROM files illegally downloaded off of the internet. Like most things in life, if you're being offered a deal at a convention and it seems too good to be true, it probably is.

- **PLAN YOUR COSPLAY AROUND THE WEATHER.** If you're going somewhere hot, it's not really recommended you dress up as the Ice Climbers from *Super Smash Bros*. Similarly, if you're going somewhere cold, you may want to leave your Wonder Woman costume at home. Cosplay is great fun, and there's not much more satisfying than dressing up as something extremely obscure and having scores of people recognize you.

- **PLAN YOUR COSTUME AROUND YOUR BODY TYPE.** In my many years of attending conventions I have, on occasion, seen a person or two dressed up in a tight or skimpy costume who really didn't have the body for it. Perhaps they were a bit too plump and had some muffin tops hanging over the sides of their pants. Or perhaps their penis was too large and protruded awkwardly from their spandex. Whatever the reason may be, try to cosplay with your body type in mind. There's a great degree of flexibility when it comes to costumes, but muffin tops and protruding penises are really only appropriate at the Muffin Top and Protruding Penis Expo.[68] On the other side, if you are blessed with a hunger for fitness or a naturally taut body, by all means feel free to show it off. Conventions can be fun, welcoming places for people to flaunt it if they've got it, so go hog-wild with your sexy outfits. If you want to show off a little more skin but aren't sure who to go as, let me help with a few suggestions.

---

[68] Held every year at the fabulous Bellagio Hotel in Las Vegas, Nevada.

Top Five Sexiest Characters to Cosplay

- **DANTE, *DEVIL MAY CRY 3*.** Dante's *DMC3* outfit is perfect for any guy looking to show off his six-pack. If you decide to go for a leather jacket, you may want to pad it a bit, because even a small amount of sweat in leather can make it chafing and uncomfortable.

- **MORRIGAN AENSLAND, *DARKSTALKERS*.** Morrigan is a succubus with curves to spare and a don't-give-a-crap attitude that makes cosplaying her a fun experience for many.

- **WEAPON X WOLVERINE.** Remember the scene from *X-Men Origins: Wolverine* where Hugh Jackman exploded out of the tank of water, murky liquid sloshing everywhere as his muscles rippled so hard they looked like they were going to pop out of his body? If you're a straight male, your answer is probably, "Sure, I guess." If you're a girl, however, your answer is probably, "Oh *yeah*."

- **YOKO LITTNER, *GURREN LAGAN*.** Yoko's default outfit is a flaming string bikini top and a pair of hot pants. If you're a girl looking to cosplay and show off some skin the only way to top Yoko is to cosplay as Naked Woman, whose power is unstoppable nudity.

- **TOM SERVO,** *MYSTERY SCIENCE THEATER 3000. MST3K*'s puppet robot Tom Servo is a beacon of raw sexuality. Bulging biceps, supportive shoulders, and legs that can leap tall buildings in a single bound—Tom's got it all!

Whenever you're deciding who to cosplay as, don't let petty things like the gender or ethnicity of the original character hold you back. If you want to go as a female Dante or an African-American Captain America, do it. When it comes to costumes, the only important thing is that you love who you're dressed up as. Feel free to get creative with it, too. Try making a steampunk or cyborg variant of your favorite character. One of the best costumes I've ever seen at a con was a steampunk girl Ash from the *Evil Dead* movies, complete with a leather bustier and a gear-powered chainsaw hand.

For the Hoard: What to Do With All That Treasure

SWAG: Stuff We All Get. Swag is neat, free stuff that gets handed out at conventions to advertise new products and to help the fans feel rewarded for coming. You'll get a lot of it at any given convention. So much so, in fact, that you may have a hard time deciding what to do with it all.

___

PAMPHLETS AND FLIERS

LOOT CLASS: G for Garbage.

Not all convention swag is created equal. For every awesome lightsaber replica or transforming car being given away, there are thousands of bits of paper plastered with the names and info of people looking to get your money. You may occasionally realize the paper you threw away had information on a party or panel you want to go to. If that's the case, go back to the person handing them out and take another one—they won't mind. The sooner they give away all of those God-forsaken fliers, the sooner they can go home.

___

BUTTONS

LOOT CLASS: D for Decent.

The value of a button depends on the person taking it. If you're not someone who likes to cover their bags in the little metal things, these buttons will just take up space. Strongly consider whether you're *really* ever going to make use of the buttons or if you only want them because they're neat.

INFLATABLE GOODS

LOOT CLASS: B for Bad, Not.

Inflatable stuff makes for nice swag. It's easy to store and take home and once you've got it all puffed up, you've got an awesome new item to show off at the pool. Some of the best inflatable items I've seen are the *Mass Effect* Omni-tool, Isaac's wire cutter from *Dead Space*, and an inflatable Vagina Dentata from *Teeth*.

CUSTOM CLOTHING

LOOT CLASS: W for Why not?

If someone is giving away clothes, take some. Doesn't matter if it's a bandanna you'll never wear or a T-shirt that's too small for you—you can always give the clothes away to your less fortunate friends who weren't able to attend the convention.

FOOD

LOOT CLASS: A for Always take.

As I've stated earlier, convention food is hard to come by. There's not much of it, the lines are long, and it's expensive. So seeing someone *giving away* food is like finding an oasis in the middle of the desert. Take as much as you can, maybe even doubling back around for seconds by changing into some of your swag clothes for a quick disguise.

ACTION FIGURES, MODELS, AND ASSORTED PLASTIC/METAL MEMORABILIA

LOOT CLASS: S for Stupid not to get as much as you can.

Clothes are good, and food is tasty, but a little plastic Optimus Prime is forever. If you see that people are giving away things in boxes, book it over to them immediately even if you're in line for free food. A meal is an ephemeral thing; you'll be hungry again later. But that sweet Rorschach limited edition figurine can sit on your desk forever glaring out at the city and refusing to save it.

DISFIGURED ANIMAL/HUMAN HYBRIDS CRYING OUT FOR THE SWEET RELEASE OF DEATH

LOOT CLASS: F for From, Run.

If you see someone giving away mutant hybrids, it's best to get the hell out of there because once the people giving them away run out of freebies, they'll probably look to refill their stock.

chapter fifteen

geeky girls

the female
is the deadlier
of the species

"Nerd girls are the world's most underutilized romantic resource. And guys, do not tell me that nerd girls are not hot because that shows a Paris Hilton-esque failure to understand hotness."
— John Green, *New York Times* Bestselling author and YouTube vlogger

Historically speaking, geekdom has been kind of a guy's club. Guys were typically the ones studying things like chemistry and medicine, while women stayed at home. But as history progressed, more women began speaking out about how much it sucked not getting to do much of anything because of their lack of a Y chromosome. After much fighting, protesting, and burning of bras, women are now treated as social and intellectual equals by anyone who isn't a complete tool. This equality has spread from the rest of society and into geekdom as well, leading to an increasing number of geek girls every year. For a deeper analysis of the phenomenon, let's turn to the history books.

History of the Geek Girl

- **600,000 BC.** The cavegeekgirl. Cavegeekgirls were an uncommon, though not entirely nonexistent, type of cave dweller. *Caveus Geekicus Girlum*, as they're scientifically called, would often have to content themselves with listening to the male cavegeeks sit around and tell tales of their male heroes, as no female heroes had been invented yet.
- **THE RENAISSANCE.** Here we see geek girl numbers increasing slowly thanks, in part, to the sheer volume of art and science being emphasized by society at this time.
- **THE 1800S.** Little in the way of American geek girl activity during this period since most women were either trying to make it as women of high society or out in the wild frontier trying not to die in childbirth or get shot to death by bandits. On the plus side, the clothes of this era help set the stage for the birth of steampunk.
- **1894.** Margaret Floy Washburn becomes the first woman to earn a PhD in psychology. After spending some time performing psychology experiments, she proclaims, "The field of psychology, as a whole, is somewhat of a sausage fest."
- **1966.** Nichelle Nichols portrays communications officer Uhura on *Star Trek*, setting a strong example for geek girls everywhere as not only a woman who was a respected member of the crew of the Enterprise, but as one of the first African-American women to portray a character in a non-subservient position.
- **1973.** Shirley Ann Jackson becomes the first African-American woman to earn a PhD in physics.
- **1988.** Ellen Ripley tells the queen alien to "Get away from her you *bitch!*" in the movie, *Aliens*.
- **1991.** Sarah Connor fights to protect her son from a machine sent back in time to kill him in *Terminator 2: Judgment Day*. Both Sigourney Weaver (Ripley) and Linda Hamilton (Connor) broke ground with their powerful performances as these equally powerful ladies.
- **1996.** Buffy the vampire slayer kills a whole lotta vampires and demons.
- **2001.** Comic book, sci-fi, and fantasy conventions see an increase in female attendees.
- **2004.** Tina Fey writes and stars in *Mean Girls*, helping transform her into an unstoppable juggernaut in the field of comedy, as well as helping highlight how flippin' mean high school girls can be.
- **2012.** Most geek conventions are now relatively even in their gender distribution, with roughly as many women as men attending.

Geek girls have had a long road to travel in their journey for acceptance amongst geek circles, and it's still not over. Many self-proclaimed enlightened geeks shy away from their female counterparts. Some do it out of fear of losing ground in a domain that has typically been a guy's club, others are guys who just feel a little awkward around the ladies and need help interacting with the fairer sex. If you're one of the latter, this next section is for you. If you're one of the former, quit being such a sexist wang.

Geek Guys: How to Not Feel So Weird Around Girls

THERE'S A FINE LINE BETWEEN CHIVALRY AND UNINTENTIONAL SEXISM. Holding a door open for a girl is generally considered to be chivalrous. Assuming a girl doesn't know how to use her Android phone because "most girls I know don't know how to use them right" is sexist. Never assume someone is incapable of doing something due to their gender or ethnicity. As Samuel L. Jackson says in the movie, *The Long Kiss Goodnight*, "You know what happens when you make an assumption—you make an ass out of U and Umption."

ACCEPT THE EXISTENCE OF GEEK GIRLS. Too often geek guys treat girls as if they're mythical, nonexistent, or alien beasts and it's just not true. Geek girls are everywhere, and they're here to stay.

DON'T CALL A GIRL'S CREDENTIALS INTO QUESTION. Countless keystrokes have been wasted on people arguing on the internet as to whether or not certain geek girls are actually *geek* girls, particularly celebrities. People, if someone says they're something when they really aren't, why does it matter? Most of the older geeks are probably scratching their head at the younger generation and thinking, "When I was in high school, I would have *killed* to have a pretty girl lie and tell me she was into *Dungeons and Dragons*." It's silly to get upset over people lying about their interests, and that's not actually the point here. You may think some people aren't *really* geeks or nerds, but thinking that doesn't make you the judge, jury, and execution when it comes to geek cred. *Being a geek shouldn't be a competition.* Just because someone knows more or less about a subject than you doesn't change their geekiness.

DON'T STARE. When an attractive girl walks by, don't stare. Women have been battling their objectification for centuries, so try to be on their side in that battle instead of against them. Similarly, don't focus on how attractive a geek girl is. If you go to Chris Hardwick's Nerdist Youtube channel, do you know what the comments say? Some nice things and some mean things, same as any other video. However, if you go to Felicia Day's Geek and Sundry Youtube channel, the comments often devolve into a discussion as to whether or not the commenters think she is attractive. These comments on her attractiveness are irrelevant and sexist. Don't do it. Don't be *that* guy. *That* guy is a total D-bag.

IF IT HELPS, YOU CAN THINK OF GIRLS AS BETTER-SMELLING BOYS ... Geek guys can get so focused on the fact that a girl is, well, a girl, they often forget to treat them like people. Maybe they'll treat them with kid gloves, letting them win a round or two of *Street Fighter* when they would have beaten the pants off of a guy in the same situation. Treat them as you would any of your guy friends ...

... TO A POINT. Being the only guy hanging out in a group of girls can get weird. The girls forget that you're a dude and end up in a discussion as to whose boyfriend is the most well-endowed, as well as detailing their menstrual cycles with such specificity you worry you'll never be able to scrub their words from your brain. This is an exaggerated example, but it doesn't mean it never happens, and when it does, it often leaves the guy feeling uncomfortable deep into his very soul. Likewise, if your group of friends is predominantly male, it's good form to remember that the few girls you're hanging out with may not love hearing what kind of "me-time" movies you like to watch or which girl at your school would look best naked. There are exceptions, of course, but in general, it's best to try to remember the kinds of topics your friends do and don't want to hear about.

Now that we've covered tips on geek guys interacting with geek girls, it's time to kickflip the subject around, '90s style, and get "real" up in here. Warning: it's going to get really real. I may even put on a backwards cap, turn a chair around, and sit in it while leaning on one elbow.

Geek Girls: How to Deal With Those Silly Boys

DON'T BE IGNORED. While geek guys may claim to be more enlightened than their athletically inclined counterparts, this isn't always the case. In science, you'll see some male scientists aggressively pursue their projects while pushing aside those of female cohorts. In fantasy role-playing games, you might see the dwarf leave the elf behind so he can kill all the orcs and claim the glory for himself. Men throughout history have been trying to keep women in the margins and it was as unacceptable then as it is now. If the guys around you aren't letting your voice be heard, then *make* it heard, even at the risk of some negative murmurs around the office/role-playing table.

DON'T FEEL LIKE YOU HAVE TO "KEEP UP" WITH THE GUYS. Whether it's headshots or pantsharts, some girls feel pressured to maintain a steady pace with their guy friends. If you're better or worse than them at something, fine. Don't try to hinder yourself/ knock yourself out so you do as well as the rest of them. Likewise, just because guys can sometimes be a bit freer with their bodily functions than girls are doesn't mean you have to as well. Only let it rip around them if you want to, not because your beefy friend William has a tendency to toot when excited.

IF YOU SENSE AN ATTRACTION BUT DON'T RECIPROCATE IT, LET THEM DOWN EASILY AND QUICKLY. Geek guys can be a sensitive breed with a proclivity toward introspection and over-thinking. While these qualities can be useful, they can also be detrimental, particularly in the case of guy-girl friendships. If you sense that one of your guy pals is attracted to you and you want to remain just friends, find ways to let him know. Some degree of bluntness may be required, and you may have to outright say something to the effect of, "I'm flattered, but I only value you as a friend, and I understand if you need some time apart after hearing this." Most guys will bounce back from this and continue with the friendship intact, but a sizable few will not react well to the news. They're called "Nice Guys" (different from regular nice guys, no capitalization, no quotations marks) and they're something that will be discussed in more detail in Chapter 16.

DON'T LET THE INCLUSION OF A NEW GIRL BE A STICKING POINT. Often geek girls will enjoy the "Penny situation," a la *The Big Bang Theory*. They thrive on being the queen bee and having all of their male bees buzzing around them. But when a new girl bee comes fluttering into the beehive, the stingers can come out and the old queen will grow threatened. Just because one of your guy friends has a new girl friend or girlfriend doesn't devalue you as a buddy. Quite the opposite—it means your social circle is expanding. Sadly, the concept of girlfights is nothing new and has actually become a surprisingly large problem for geek girls around the world.

Girl vs. Girl: When the Controllers are Down, the Adamantium Claws Come Out

Oddly enough, geek girls are often the group most critical of other geek girls, perhaps feeling threatened by virtue of no longer being the only lady around. This is a trend that *must* stop. It makes it tough for new girls to want to enter the geeky fold and it makes everyone involved look petty and mean. Here are some things to look out for to realize when a geek girl is being nasty toward you or when you might actually be the one being nasty without realizing it.

CALLING A GEEK GIRL'S CREDENTIALS INTO QUESTION. I bring up this point again because it's so, *so* important. The overwhelming thing I've heard and been told by geek girls is that they get tired of *other* geek girls trying to call them out on not being geeky. My basic points from earlier apply: If someone is more or less geeky than you, it's all good. Don't make it a sticking point. Likewise, if someone claims to be into something when they aren't (which, in all honestly, doesn't happen very often), who friggin' cares? Let them say they like it. They may even lie about it for so long that they become interested and learn about it on their own.

> "As an adult, I realize this girl-on-girl sabotage is the third worst kind of female behavior, right behind saying 'like' all the time and leaving your baby in a dumpster."
> — Tina Fey, *Bossypants*

DISCOUNTING PHYSICALLY ATTRACTIVE GEEK GIRLS. At the San Diego Comic-Con 2011, Action Chick Katrina Hill headed up a convention panel titled, "Oh, You Sexy Geek!" a discussion on whether it is demeaning for a geek girl to be sexy in her cosplay, and how often the opinion of geek girls gets devalued if the geek girl is physically attractive. Ultimately, many of the panelists leaned toward sexy cosplay being A-OK if it makes the girl wearing the costume feel empowered. Both points were sources of much contention, so much so there were even bloggers who later complained about the lack of unattractive females on the panel and rejected the panelists' opinions because the bloggers felt they were too attractive, which is *exactly what the discussion was about in the first place.* Young or old, fat or skinny, ugly or pretty: geekdom knows no physical bounds. To discount someone because you think they're too fit or too good-looking is small-minded and petty. Don't let yourself fall into that trap. Instead, try to be an inspiration to your fellow geek girls like the ladies in this next section.

Ladies Who Set a Good Example

TINA FEY. Comedy, it's often said, is kind of a boy's club, as is the entertainment industry. So when Tina Fey became the first female head writer at *Saturday Night Live* it was *kind* of a big deal. Fey spent several years at *SNL* writing skits and co-hosting the Weekend Update segments with the ever-giggling Jimmy Fallon. Eventually, Fey graduated from *SNL* and began working on her own film and television career, starring in the highly successful television series *30 Rock,* as well as box-office smashes like *Mean Girls, Date Night,* and *Megamind.*

FELICIA DAY. It'd be tough to find a better geek girl role model than Felicia Day. She began college at age 16 and graduated valedictorian with a double major in mathematics and music performance. From there, she went into acting, earning a role as potential slayer Vi on the final season of *Buffy the Vampire Slayer* before eventually creating her own web series, *The Guild,* a series that since caught fire and exploded like a mad scientist's invention gone awry. Felicia Day is a self-made geek empire, proving to any and all that great things can happen for those with the tenacity to *make* them happen.

OPRAH WINFREY. By many accounts, Oprah Winfrey is one of, if not the, most powerful women in the world. There are islands in the South Pacific where natives sacrifice pigs in the name of the great one, Oh-Prah, in the hopes that her benevolence will rain down on them. Oprah Winfrey once stopped a charging bull with naught but a severe look in her eye. Since the 1990s, Oprah has been a household name, acting as not only a talk show host, but philanthropist and media proprietor.

JANE GOODALL. The world's foremost expert on chimpanzees, Jane Goodall is a primatologist, anthropologist, and all-around nice lady. Her research on primates has not only helped us further understand our evolutionary cousins, but helped us to understand our own behavior.

CAMILA BATMANGHELIDJH. Ms. Batman has a long last name and an even longer list of charities she has helped found and organize over the years, perhaps the most famous of which being Kids Company, a charity designed to help juvenile delinquents and inner-city kids get centered and on track to do something positive with their lives. It's no surprise that Camila has gone on to do such selfless work. After all, the middle of her name *is* Batman.

WANGARI MAATHAI. Ms. Maathai was world-renowned for her works in environmentalism and political activism, eventually earning a Nobel Peace Prize for her contributions to the preservation of the environment, democracy, and general peace.

MAYA ANGELOU. Born Marguerite Ann Johnson, Maya Angelou is a poet and author whose works have inspired generations of writers around the globe. She's credited with being one of the first memoirists to highlight the plight of African-Americans during the civil rights movement of the 1960s, and through her work she's helped spread cultural awareness and acceptance across the U.S.

J.K. ROWLING. Odds are good that if you're reading this book, you don't need me to explain who J.K. Rowling is. However, I'm going to explain it anyway because it's my book and I can do whatever I want. J.K. Rowling is a novelist best known for a little series about a kid named Harry Potter who learns magic. No big deal, the novels are only the *best-selling book series in history.* They've also been adapted into movies that made a couple of bucks on the side. An entire generation learned to read on *Harry Potter*, growing alongside the character from children to adults, and thanks to the success of the series, Rowling has blossomed into a respected writer and philanthropist.

Real life isn't the only place to find inspirational women—for years, writers have created fictional ladies who excel at badassery and who have left a lasting legacy in the minds of impressionable youths everywhere.

Fiction's Most Badass Action Chicks

CHARACTER: Wonder Woman.

SOURCE MATERIAL: *All Star Comics* #8; *Sensation Comics* #1.

BACKGROUND: Created by William Moulton Marston, inventor of the lie detector,

Wonder Woman became the feminine answer to the countless depictions of masculine strength in popular culture. She's strong, determined, and doesn't need a man to get things done. While nowadays the image of a powerful female is a bit more prevalent, in the 1940s it was a rarity. Wonder Woman helped set the stage for the strong women who followed her by establishing that women could be independent and powerful without having to sacrifice their femininity.

CHARACTER: Ellen Ripley.

SOURCE MATERIAL: The *Alien* film series.

BACKGROUND: The first *Alien* film ends with Ripley (Sigourney Weaver) as the lone survivor of a malevolent space creature's bloody rampage, having lived by virtue of her wits and determination. In the second film, we see a changed Ripley, one hardened by the things she's seen. She spends the early part of the film surrounded by hyper-masculine characters who constantly scoff at her claims and try to silence her. When a space colony gets besieged by the alien creatures that dismembered Ripley's crew from the first film, she finds the only survivor: a little girl named Newt. Ripley's struggles to both survive the alien attackers, make her voice heard, and to protect Newt all exemplify the struggles women often experience when trying to get their opinions heard in an over-masculinized world, as well as exemplifying the way that women can show strength while balancing out qualities which are both traditionally masculine and feminine.

Buffy at the salon.

CHARACTER: Buffy Summers.

SOURCE MATERIAL: *Buffy the Vampire Slayer* film and television series.

BACKGROUND: Throughout the '80s and '90s, most slasher films opened with the same kind of scene: brain-dead blonde gets cut to pieces by some bloodthirsty killer. Joss Whedon dreamed up the character of Buffy the Vampire Slayer (played on TV by Sarah Michelle Gellar and in the movie by Kristy Swanson) when watching one such film and thinking to himself, "How cool would it be if this girl turned around and kicked the crap out of the bad guy?" Buffy is altogether hard and soft; she's powerful and takes orders from no one, but she's got plenty of doubts about herself, as well as a love of high fashion.

CHARACTER: Sarah Connor.

SOURCE MATERIAL: The *Terminator* film series, *Terminator: the Sarah Connor Chronicles* television series.

BACKGROUND: You know how it is—one day you meet a guy, he tells you that machines are going to revolt and destroy humanity, that your unborn son is going to lead the resistance against them, and that the machines have sent terminators back in time to kill you and him. We've all heard *that* pick-up line before. But in the case of Sarah Connor (Linda Hamilton in the films; Lena Heady on TV), it was actually true, and she spends the rest of her days on the run, preparing for the inevitable worst. Sarah Connor may well be the world's toughest mom—few mothers are bottle-feeding a baby with one hand while reloading a machine

TriStar Pictures/Heritage Auctions

gun with the other. Sarah Connor has devoted her life to making sure her kid survives and it's an ideal that many parents, particularly single parents, can readily identify with. It's hard being a parent, requiring countless sacrifices your kids will never know about or understand. Of course, being a parent is a *little* harder for Sarah Connor seeing as how there are time traveling androids who want her and her kid dead.

CHARACTER: Xena.

SOURCE MATERIAL: *Hercules: the Legendary Journeys* and *Xena: Warrior Princess* television series.

BACKGROUND: Outlaw-turned-hero, Xena the warrior princess (Lucy Lawless) is an

Renaissance Pictures

ass-kicker of the highest degree. She and her "companion" Gabrielle (Renée O'Connor) traveled the lands of Ancient Greece searching for injustices to justice-ify. Not only was the character a paragon of female power, but she provided an important role model to the lesbian community thanks to her ambiguously gay relationship with her partner-in-crime-preventing, Gabrielle.

CHARACTER: Samus Aran.

SOURCE MATERIAL: *Metroid* video game series.

BACKGROUND: In the 1986 Nintendo game *Metroid*, you play as Samus Aran, a bounty hunter equipped with a high-tech suit of armor. Most games of the time featured male heroes and so, when players are first shown the image of this gun-toting, armor-clad character, many assumed that character was male. It's only after completing the game do we see Samus sans-helmet, her hair flowing in the space winds for all to enjoy. More than twenty-five years later, Samus is still a character who resonates with players male and female alike. Something about her stoicism, her self-reliance, and her sweet-ass set of power armor makes people want to play as her to explore the most decrepit, most lonely reaches of the galaxy. Samus is to video game heroines what Wonder Woman is for comic book heroines: she set the stage for those who followed her.

Samus at the salon.

I'm often asked to trace back the origin of my nerdiness, as if I was hit by gamma rays or bitten by a radioactive spider. No single event can capture how I turned nerd. I've always considered "being nerdy" a personality trait that begins in childhood, like an inborn characteristic that draws certain people to read comic books, collect action figures, play hours and hours of board games, or become lost in fantastical worlds in galaxies far, far away.

It's not so much *what* we are drawn to, but our *obsessive-like fascination and irrepressible passion* about a topic that makes us geeky. At a young age, I attached to nerdy things via the gateway of television. As if to escape the most awkward phase of adolescence, I rushed home every day after school to watch *Batman: The Animated Series*. When I first discovered Bruce Timm's stylized, dark version of the Caped Crusader, a long-term relationship formed that could never be disrupted. The following years included collections of comic books, graphic novels, DVDs, action figures, and anything related to Batsy.

But it wasn't Batman alone who fueled my obsession. Batman's mission is to rid Gotham City of the evil that took his parents' lives—for there to be continued stories about the Great Detective, villains must exist. Batman stories are ostensibly about Bruce Wayne's recovery from the murder of his parents, his struggle with his more heroic alter-ego, his underlying need to connect with others. However, I considered most Batman narratives to be villain-centered. What drew me to the comics, films, and video games were the awesome and dynamic villains getting thrown in and breaking out of Arkham Asylum. "What makes them *crazy*? What drove them to thievery, violence, murder?" My nerdiness stems from my relentless questions about assassins, psychopaths, maniacs, and evil-doers—my earliest obsession surrounded the baddies of Gotham City's Rogue's Gallery.

— *Dr. Andrea Letamendi, PhD*

geek love
the fifth element

Geek love and the
abandoned pillow.

> "Gravitation can not be held responsible for people falling in love."
> — Albert Einstein

There's a reason the 1997 Bruce Willis documentary *The Fifth Element* portrays love as being one of the five basic elements: it's as basic to our survival as water or air. Whether it's the love of your family, your friends, or that special someone waiting for you at the end of the day, it's something we all need. If you've already got a good family and a fun group of friends to call your own but still feel like you're missing something, then maybe it's time to venture into the most dangerous realm of all: the world of dating.

Think of dating like an adventure on another planet. Sometimes you'll see amazing new things, such as the smile of a beautiful girl or a waterfall that flows up instead of down, but other times you'll be scared and confused, like when your blind date shows up and he insists he go on the date "in character" as Grandpa Munster. Dating can be a terrifying prospect, which is why I've compiled a handy list of tips to follow when trying to navigate this strange and exciting world.

Ways to Have Fun While Dating and Not Accidentally End Up On a Date With a Person Who is Secretly an Evil Robot or Something

- Meeting potential dates can be tough; most couples end up meeting through school, work, or mutual friends. If you're looking to date someone, you could first try asking around with your friends to see if they know anyone who is available. Be wary of dates set up by any of your more prank-oriented friends, as they may stick you with someone who is fugly or a velociraptor in disguise and, trust me, being eviscerated by your date in the bathroom of an Arby's is not the way you want your evening to go.

- Study what people in romantic-comedies do, and don't do any of them. Rom-coms exist in some sort of bizarre quasi-universe populated with one-dimensional people who run around spouting quippy lines with their gay best friends who are always conveniently available to bitch with. Women are overworked and underappreciated, while men are all muscular playboys. Neither of these is universally true in the real world. While, yes, there are people who may fit these stereotypes, you're going to find far more people who're more interesting than these vapid shells, so don't use them as role models.

- Attention from someone of the opposite gender does not always equal attraction. Human attraction is a tricky thing; there's a reason I've devoted this entire chapter to it. Let me give you an example of a sad story that's all too common: a guy and a girl end up becoming friends. The girl thinks they're buds and has a blast staying up late with her new pal talking about her past while they watch every episode of *Arrested Development*; the guy mistakes this attention for attraction and gets frustrated when the girl begins dating someone else. This is a clear misfire of communication, and one that's not easily remedied. That's right, you heard me. There's no easy way to tell when people are attracted to you. There are some fairly universal signs when it comes to interactions, with things like touching, making eye contact, smiling, and turning knees toward you being generally good signs, while things like crossed arms, turning away from you, and screaming at the sight of you being bad. Regardless of these general rules, however, no two people act completely alike. Sometimes if you're into someone, you have to go for it and hope for the best.

- Pop quiz: what is the number one most universally attractive quality for a person to have? Confidence. People like being around people with confidence. If you go around putting yourself down all the time and saying you're worthless, guess what? People are going to believe it. How people see you is defined by you, not them, so go out there with confidence. Believe in yourself! You're awesome and it's time you let everyone else know exactly how awesome you are.

- Being nice to someone does not entitle you to date them. It seems odd to have to say this, but there seems to have been an increase in the amount of self-described "Nice Guys" who are only nice to a girl in the hopes she'll date them. Women are not dating machines you can put kindness tokens into and out pop sex tickets. When being nice to someone, you should evaluate whether you're being nice because you genuinely like the person or because all you want is to hook up with them.

- Make your intentions clear. Dating is a bizarre game of coy comments and hidden meanings; it can be frustrating when one person thinks the date went well but the other doesn't call afterwards. People do this because they don't want to look foolish—no one likes putting themselves out there only to be rejected. Still, using some measure of directness can help your relationship bloom more easily rather than having to resort to rom-com-style double talk.[69]

- On rare occasions, you may find that you're on a date not with a human being, but an evil android masquerading as a person. If you're on the ropes about your date possibly being of the metal and sparks variety rather than flesh and blood, consult these handy guidelines:

  *Has your date eaten? It's tough for robots to eat, but not impossible, so if they've eaten you can relax … a little.

  *Are your date's movements stiff and unnatural? Does his or her expression seem unsettling? Do their eyes shine with a plastic luster?

  *Ask your date to divide by zero, or say, "This statement is false." If his/her head explodes, he/she was probably a robot.

  *Does your date occasionally power down and become listless, unable to be roused from what appears to be a brief coma? Robot.

  *Does your date have superhuman strength, endurance, and durability? Do his/her limbs transform into weapons, either projectile or melee? Does their skin peel off to reveal a metallic endoskeleton underneath? If you've answered yes to the first question, your date may be a superhero, which would be a plus. If

---

[69] And when I say "be honest," I mean "be honest to a certain extent." It's good to tell someone that you do or do not like them romantically. It is bad form to say to someone, "I don't really care about what you're saying, but you fill out those pants very nicely and I'd like to see them on my floor with you on top of me."

There are many questions you can ask yourself to make sure you're not dating a robot in disguise.

you've answered yes to either of the other two, your date is probably a robot, and also probably computing the most efficient way to destroy you so you don't reveal its identity to anyone else. What I'm trying to say is that you should put down the book and RUN! Get out of the restaurant right now!

What kind of person should you date? That's up to you. Just because you are or are not geeky doesn't limit you to dating other geeks or non-geeks. After all, many of histories greatest romances have been between geeks and non-geeks. But let's be honest— sometimes it's better to date geeks.

Top Five Reasons It's Better to Date Geeks

1. YOU'LL GET EACH OTHER'S REFERENCES. Have you ever come up with the perfect joke or to realize halfway through it that the other person has a zero percent chance of getting the reference?[70] It's not a fun feeling, but when you're dating a fellow geek, you

---

[70] For example, at a family gathering, one of the babies began crying and wouldn't stop. When his mother put a pacifier in his mouth, I laughed and said that it was "Super effective!" She just gave me a very strange look and said, "Yeah, I guess it was," before hurrying off with her baby.

can rest easy that they'll get your references. Probably not *all* of them, unless you two have somehow only ever seen the same movies and TV shows, which would imply that you were perhaps long-lost fraternal twins, and in that case, you may want to stop dating.

2. THEY GET THE CONCEPT OF "ALONE TIME." It's finally here. After months of waiting, *Diablo III*/the new iPad/your robot dog has arrived and all you want to do is sit down and spend the next few hours engrossed with it. If you're dating a geek, they'll understand and give you some space. Non-geeks, however, may not get what the big deal is and may leave you alone for twenty minutes or so, but after half an hour, they won't understand why you're still tinkering with this new gadget when you could be doing something they consider productive, like cleaning your home or taking a shower.

3. YOU'LL HAVE SOMEONE WITH WHOM TO SHARE YOUR NERD RAGE. This just in: Michael Bay is going to adapt *Doctor Who* for the big screen! This is a new *Who*, darker and edgier than ever before. Instead of being a benevolent genius traveling through time and space, he's a rapping robot built by the United States Military to battle D.A.L.E.K., a supergenius alien played by Shia LaBeouf. If the thought of a rapping, robotic, non-doctor Doctor Who didn't send chills down your spine, I don't know what will. The point

> "Love makes you do the wacky."
> — Willow, *Buffy the Vampire Slayer*

behind that morbid exercise was that if, Thor forbid, that headline actually *were* real, when dating a geek you'd have someone to share your outrage with, as well as someone who will understand why it's now your mission to buy plane tickets to Los Angeles and spray-paint the words STINK BUTT on Michael Bay's car in protest.

4. GEEKS ARE SMARTER, BETTER READ, AND BETTER EDUCATED. Well, most of the time. Dumb geeks are rare, but they do happen. Just look at *Saved by the Bell*'s Screech—the guy can build a robot, but can't make the tiniest leaps in social logic? Sure he ended up valedictorian at Bayside High, but when your school consists of six teens and around a dozen mute background students, it's not too hard to have the best grades around.

5. YOU WON'T HAVE TO GO TO CONVENTIONS ALONE. Conventions entail a *lot* of waiting. Waiting in line to get your badge, waiting in line to get to a panel, waiting to get to the line for the Waiting In Line For Panels panel. It's exhausting. If you've got someone with you, the wait is much easier. You've got a partner for conversation, you can play a few games to pass the time, and if you really have to tinkle, you'll know your spot's been saved.

Tips for Dating a Geek

MOVIES ALWAYS MAKE FOR GOOD DATES. If you enjoy it, great! If not, the two of you can spend dinner afterwards discussing how said movie destroyed your childhood.

STAYING IN IS OFTEN A GEEK'S FAVORITE OPTION. Now I'm not saying you shouldn't take your special lady/man friend out for a night on the town once in a while, but if you're feeling cozy or if money's tight, geeks are usually happy to stay in and watch a few movies, or spend a few hours going back through your favorite TV shows. Or if you're looking to expand your perspectives, there are a few peculiar documentaries you can find online, things like *Word Wars*, which chronicles the journey of four semi-professional *Scrabble* players as they prep for a major *Scrabble* tournament, or *Monster Camp*, a documentary about a group of LARPers, or even *The Rock-afire Explosion*, which tells the tale of the eponymous animatronic band formerly featured in the Showbiz Pizza chain before it became a part of Chuck E. Cheese.

EMBRACE THE THINGS YOU HAVE IN COMMON, AND RESPECT THE THINGS YOU DON'T. As evidenced by the Know Your Geeks section in the first chapter, there are a wide range of topics that geeks can geek out over. You and your geeky lover will probably have a few in common (or else you may not end up dating for long), but there will probably also be some things you don't agree on. Maybe she's into *D&D* and you're not, or maybe you secretly *love* Jar-Jar Binks and she thinks he should be nuked from orbit.[71] Regardless of what your differences are, you need to respect them no matter how much you do or do not understand them. This goes for any couple, really, not just geeky ones.

If you've managed to begin dating a fellow geek, hopefully things are going well. And if you're dating a non-geek, that's peachy, too. With any luck, the two of you can help expose each other to all kinds of new things and broaden each other's horizons. That's part of the fun of dating—you become so intimately familiar with another person that often *their* interests will become *your* interests and each of you will become more cultured people.

This is a good thing ... usually. There are a few topics and ideas that, if either of you are *really* into, perhaps it's best you don't spread them around. I'm not talking about religion, or whether or not the new *Battlestar Galactica* was a *great* TV series or the *greatest* TV series. No, I'm talking about dark things, the kinds of things you'd rather not have your Gramma know about. I'm talking about ... fetishes.

Fetishes: Oddball Fetishes Geek Culture has Propagated

Keep in mind that the following discussion of fetishes isn't to demean, it's to educate. A fetish is, by its very nature, something that is out of the ordinary, so just because we're discussing how unusual these things are doesn't mean we judge you for enjoying them. You pervert.

Furries

Many people enjoy sexy-times with their loved one (or ones). Some will dress up in erotic outfits to spice things up in the bedroom. Things like lingerie are pretty common, although sometimes you'll encounter specialty outfits at costume stores, like Sexy Nurse, Sexy Maid, or Sexy High School Textbook Proofreader. But for some people, it's not enough to pretend to be a different person while having an erotic encounter. For these folks, what they *really* want is to be a different *species*. Believe it or not, there are people who enjoy pretending they're wolves or giraffes while doing the deed.

This isn't to be confused with regular furries—those are people who pretend they're

---

[71] She's right, you know. If you do love Jar-Jar, then shame on you!

animal-people on online forums or at conventions. Furry fetishists take this one step further by only being aroused by the thoughts of animal-people getting it on. *The Lion King* is foreplay to them. Other innocent films such as *101 Dalmatians* or *Madagascar* suddenly become breeding grounds for people to fantasize about having sex with 101 spotted people or hippopotami.

Hentai

Ahh, Japan. Source of much of what is weird and wonderful in this world. Part of that strangeness stems from how polite and occasionally repressed Japanese society is, and it is a strangeness which spills over into their erotica. For those who aren't in the know, hentai is like regular anime (a Japanese cartoon style), only it features people doing it. If you're lucky, it will *just* be people having sex. Some hentai takes full advantage of the animated medium to show all sorts of imaginative and horrifying versions of sex, including, but not limited to: evil demons molesting schoolgirls, evil sea creatures molesting schoolgirls, evil machines molesting schoolgirls, and schoolgirls molesting schoolgirls, with or without the evilness.

Parody porn

Pornographic parodies of established intellectual properties has long been a blooming subset of the pornographic world, but with the propagation of the "ironic internet" generation, it's found a new audience. You've got XXX knockoffs of everything from *The Avengers* to *Star Trek* to *The Simpsons*. In case you're wondering, yes, the actors had their skin spray-painted yellow using non-toxic body spray and yes, it looks as weird and creepy as it sounds.

Fan fiction

We geeks love the things we love with a *passion,* and are ever-hungry for new material. While most of us have to be content to sit around waiting for the next episode or issue featuring our favorite characters, there are those out there who will take a more ... creative approach and write their *own* stories. Sometimes these stories are harmless creative exercises, such as a twelve-year-old penning a poorly written rendition of what her life would be like if she lived on the starship Serenity. Other times they take a more disturbing direction with their stories, imagining what it would be like if *Firefly's* Mal and Wash got married. And Wash, through some bizarre future science, got pregnant. And the baby was secretly Shepard Book's.

Try googling the names of two of your favorite characters together and I guarantee you'll find erotically charged stories or clumsily drawn illustrations of these characters locked in sexual situations. No one is sure where the first bit of fan fiction came from, but many internet historians theorize it featured a Kirk X Spock pairing; a speculative tale filling in the lines in these two friends' relationship with a homosexual undertone. Sometimes these unusual bits of fiction can be extremely beneficial—they can be very funny, or provide a unique perspective on characters who have become well-worn in popular culture. But most of the time the writing is poor, the characterization weak, and the sex stuff gets really weird. *Really* weird.

Sonic stuff

Sonic the Hedgehog was Sega's video game mascot in the 1990s. The blue speedster moved like the wind and had attitude coming out of his ass. He starred in a number of hit games, all of which were colorful affairs filled with creative levels and groovy music. But then technology kept advancing and Sonic had difficulty adjusting to the times. Since the '90s, he's been in a slew of poorly received games, with critics rating most of them as "pure garbage" at worst to "partial garbage" at best.

Enter 2012. Only the most devoted of Sonic fans remain. Some have clung to Sonic's glory days on the Sega Genesis, thinking only of the good times. Others have begun filling in the gaps, writing their own strange fan fiction, or drawing *bizarre* fan art. Like Sonic and Tails? Want to see them in a threesome with Tai from *Digimon*, with Knuckles the Echidna watching in the corner, videotaping the whole affair and smoking a cigar? You *wouldn't* want to see that? Of course not. No one wants to see that, not even the people drawing it.

Once your respective fetishes have been dealt with, things are going pretty well between you and your geeky lover. You spend all of your time together, you talk about each other constantly when apart, you're so cloyingly in love that you make everyone around you fight the urge to vomit. Spending your life with anyone else isn't an option anymore, leaving you with only two choices: a murder/suicide pact or getting married. Since murder/suicide pacts are thoroughly yucky affairs, I'd suggest you lean toward marriage, but hey, that's your call. If you do take the high road and begin your journey to matrimonial bliss, know that it's a road fraught with as little or as much peril as you want it to be. But before you hear the ringing of those wedding bells, you'll have to pick your best man/maid of honor, get some "bridesmaids and groomsmen" and, most importantly, have a bachelor/bachelorette party.

Throwing a Geeky Bachelor/Bachelorette Party

If you're the person getting married, this section is, honestly, not for you. But if you're the best man/maid of honor (two titles which will henceforth be collectively referred to as the Awesome Captain), it's your job to throw the most butt-bombingly fun party you can muster.

- **DO** listen to what the bride or groom wants. If they say they want a nice, quiet evening with a few friends sitting around drinking margaritas, then so be it. Don't secretly hire a twenty-man rap group to perform in their living room unless you're *really* sure it's what your friend wants. Too many bachelor/bachelorette parties have been ruined by the Awesome Captain assuming that they have to do what everyone else does at these types of shindigs, rather than thinking about who their target audience is.

- **DON'T** do anything illegal (unless it's really cool).

- **DON'T** expect your party to be "exactly like *The Hangover*." You'll probably end up disappointed and missing a few teeth.

- **TREAT** exotic dancers with respect. If you decide to hire one of the many fine exotic dancers available to entertain you and your friends, remember that they're people, not ornaments, and while it's okay to hoot and holler, it's not okay to be disrespectful. Examine the following scenarios and use your judgment to determine whether or not they're okay.

    SCENARIO A: The exotic dancer is giving you a lap dance and you gently place a bill in that person's g-string.

    SCENARIO B: You heckle the exotic dancer without mercy, demeaning their choices of songs and vocation.

    SCENARIO C: Your exotic dancer has arrived and before two words have been exchanged, you've torn off a section of his/her shirt and said, "AHH! FRESH MEAT!"

    SCENARIO D: There is no bachelor party. You've hired the exotic dancer to trick that person into going through a brutal series of *Saw*-style trap rooms. As the dancer traverses your labyrinth of terror, he/she finds the skeletal remains of a pizza boy and you cackle ominously through the speakers and say, "I ASKED FOR

CHEESY BREAD, NOT BREADSTICKS. SOMEONE HAD TO PAY."

The correct answers? A is appropriate; B, C, and *especially* D are not.[72] If you're not sure about appropriate etiquette you can always ask the exotic dancer what they're comfortable with. They'll probably appreciate the fact that you're trying to make the experience as comfortable and fun for them as it is for you. Remember who this is all about. As the Awesome Captain, it's your job to throw your best bud a great party even if you don't particularly feel like it. Maybe you're bummed that your friend is getting married and you're still single, or maybe you're still feeling loopy after having freshly been brought back from the dead via a blasphemous science experiment. Whatever the reason, you have to check your ego at the door, hang up your hangups on the coat rack, and show your best friend the party that he or she deserves.

- **DON'T** go to a Tijuana Donkey Show, or any Donkey Show for that matter. While it may sound funny in theory, the reality of the thing is that it's an ugly, hairy affair, something so shame-inducing that after it's over, none of the audience members will be able to look each other in the eye for a while.

Once the bachelor and bachelorette parties have ended, the time comes to take that final step: actually getting married. Most couples have traditional style weddings, with the bride dressed in white, guys in tuxedos, and bridesmaids in dresses designed specifically to make them look way less attractive than the bride.

However, the more creative couples out there may take it upon themselves to come up with a special theme for their wedding. Some of the themes are just sad, like the redneck couple, who had a shotgun-themed wedding, complete with beer cans everywhere, a wedding party dressed in camouflage, and a pregnant bride.

Other couples, however, tap into their creativity and common interests to come up with something really special.

---

[72] Good Lord is D not appropriate. If you thought it was, you may want to get some counseling and stay the heck away from me.

The Top Five Best Geeky Wedding Themes

5. Getting Married Episode I: A New Hope

BRIDE: Princess Leia. For classier affairs, go with Death Star Leia in her white robes, with or without her cinnamon-roll hairstyle. For a wedding that's a little on the funkier side, go with *Jedi*'s Slave Leia in the gold bikini.

GROOM: Han Solo frozen in carbonite. Find a giant block of Styrofoam and spray paint it black, carving the groom's frozen face and body into the front, and then attach the groom to the back for the big day.

MAID OF HONOR: You can either go with a Queen Padme outfit a la the *Star Wars* prequels or if you prefer to keep things within the same trilogy, go with a gold dress for a C-3PO vibe.

BEST MAN: A blue and white tux will give him that R2-D2 look he so craves.

BRIDESMAIDS: Sexy stormtroopers.

GROOMSMEN: Wookies.

WEDDING OFFICIAL: Darth Vader. Try not to mess up your vows or your wedding official may Force-choke the life out of you.

DECORATIONS: Imperial and rebel insignias.

WEDDING MARCH: *Imperial March* by John Williams.

4. Wedding in the Mushroom Kingdom

BRIDE: Princess Peach. Outside of any Mario sports games, Peach wears a very large, very poofy pink dress with heels, an outfit perfect for any bride.

GROOM: Mario. Red and blue tuxedo. If the groom cannot grow as luxurious of a 'stache as Mario, have him wear a fake one or shame him publicly.

MAID OF HONOR: Daisy. Large, yellow dress.

BEST MAN: Luigi. Both Daisy and Luigi are perfect counterparts to the bride's and groom's Peach and Mario—much like the characters themselves, the Maid of Honor and Best Man are there to play second banana and make their counterparts look better by comparison.

BRIDESMAIDS: Goombas. The bridesmaids should wear regular dresses but attach bushy black eyebrows to their faces and try to look angry.

GROOMSMEN: Mushroom kingdom citizens. Puffy white pants, blue vests, red and white mushroom hats, and no shirts.

Star Wars Wedding.

WEDDING OFFICIAL: Bowser. Try to find a wedding official who can breathe fire to really bring the character to life.

DECORATIONS: Green and red mushrooms.

WEDDING MARCH: *World 1-1 (Aboveground Theme)* by Koji Kando.

3. Uncanny X-Wedding

BRIDE: Jean Grey. You've got a number of outfits to work with here, but it's recommended you go with Jean Grey's Phoenix outfit rather than her Marvel Girl outfit, as the Marvel Girl obscured her face and looked kind of doofy in general.

GROOM: Cyclops. Throw on a pair of red sunglasses and a tuxedo and call it a day.

MAID OF HONOR: Storm. This works best if your maid of honor happens to be African-American. If she isn't, insist she dye her hair white and talk in an African accent so people will understand who she's supposed to be.

BEST MAN: Wolverine. Don't let your best man shave for a few days before the wedding, and style his hair into The Wolverine (see page 35). When the wedding official gets to the "speak now or forever hold your peace" part of the ceremony, be sure everyone knows to look to the best man with an "oh snap!" face to get his reaction.

BRIDESMAIDS: '90s Jubilee. Yellow raincoats, pink sunglasses, and blue shorts. Ain't nothin' classier.

GROOMSMEN: Gambit. Why should the bridesmaids get to be the only ones wearing coats?

WEDDING OFFICIAL: Professor X. If your wedding official isn't bald, pin him down and shave him like a wild pig.

DECORATIONS: The Xavier's School for Gifted Youngster's X insignia.

WEDDING MARCH: *X-Men Animated Series Theme* by Shuki Levy and Ron Wasserman *or*, if you've got a taste for the esoteric and ironic, you can go with Rob Walsh's opening theme to *Pryde of the X-Men*, the unaired pilot to the 1989 *X-Men* cartoon.

2. Lord of the Weddings

BRIDE: Arwyn. If your bride prefers to be a pretty princess on her big day, Arwyn had more than a few beautiful dresses in the *LotR* trilogy or she can don Arwyn's outfit from *The Fellowship of the Ring* to get a nice battle maiden look.

GROOM: Aragorn. Maybe take a bath beforehand, though, because Aragorn tended to look a little dirty.[73]

MAID OF HONOR: Aeowyn. Have her walk the bride down the aisle before the ceremony and then, when the wedding official asks who will give away the bride, have her rip off her helmet to exclaim, "I AM NO MAN!" before punching the wedding official in the face.

BEST MAN: Frodo. It's only right that the bearer of the one ring should bear the ring at your wedding.

BRIDESMAIDS: Ring Wraiths. Hard for the bridesmaids to outshine the bride if they look like the black riders of Mordor. Those guys are freakin' *grim*.

GROOMSMEN: Dwarfs. If you've got the money, make them go through the full John Rhys-Davies and put on facial prosthetics and fake beards.

WEDDING OFFICIAL: Gandalf. Try to find the oldest wedding official you can. Extra points if he's late to the wedding.

DECORATIONS: Rings and volcanoes.

WEDDING MARCH: *The Road Goes Ever On* (*The Lord of the Rings* main theme) by Howard Shore.

---

[73] For a gay wedding of any kind, the bride and bride or groom and groom can dress up as Frodo and Sam. And *LotR* purists needn't worry about what is or isn't canonical; in all honesty, Frodo and Sam were about two Meaningful Glances away from French-kissing on the craggy rocks of Mt. Doom.

1. Wedding of Justice

BRIDE: Wonder Woman. This costume may be the easiest for the bride, as Wonder Woman already comes accessorized with some snazzy wristbands and a badass tiara.

GROOM: Batman or Superman, bride's choice.

MAID OF HONOR: Black Canary or Zatanna, depending on whether your maid of honor can sing or is good at stage magic. If she's good as neither, let her go as Catwoman but make her steal the cat costume.

BEST MAN: The Flash or Green Lantern. Exactly *which* Flash or Green Lantern is up to you. Me, I prefer the classic Barry Allen/Hal Jordan team.

BRIDESMAIDS: Swamp Thing. It may seem cruel to dress your bridesmaids as a borderline undead plant creature, but remember that it's their job to make the bride look more beautiful by comparison, and if this means that they have to be swamp monsters, so be it.

GROOMSMEN: Superboy if the groom is dressed as Superman, Robin if the groom is dressed as Batman.

WEDDING OFFICIAL: The Joker. Beware wedding officials who get too into the role, however, as they may fill the room with nitrous oxide so that the ceremony is "funnier."

DECORATIONS: Wonder Woman Ws, Superman Ss, or bat logos.

WEDDING MARCH: *Wonder Woman* opening theme by Charles Fox and Norman Gimbel. As the newlyweds are marching out of the chapel, you can either play the *Superman* theme by John Williams or the *Batman* theme by Danny Elfman, depending on who your groom is.

Congratulations! You've found your one true love, punched the demons of spinsterhood in the face, and are now happily married! Being married to a geek is similar to dating one, only you see each other more. So long as both of you allow each other the appropriate amount of space and slack, everything should hit a peaceful equilibrium ... unless something throws it off. I'm talking about a force of pure chaos, something so unrelentingly demanding that you can't help but cater to its whims. I speak, of course of ... a *baby.*

raising them
right

how to forge little geeks of your own

> "Luckily, growing up 'unfinished' can make geeks the very best people
> to guide and nurture the next generation of outsiders:
> We know you don't have to be finished to be awesome."
> — Stephen H. Segal, *Geek Wisdom: The Sacred Teachings of Nerd Culture*

O utside of discovering that you are the Slayer or secretly the Anti-Christ, few things are as monumentally life-changing as having a baby. They're whiny, they're needy, they cost a *fortune* ... but they're so darn cute.

If you decide kids are a venue you want to explore, you'll have your work cut out for you; there's a whole slew of things you'll need to study and prepare before the arrival of the chosen one. Outside of mundane things like assembling a crib or painting murals of your favorite *Starcraft 2* matches on the wall of your baby's room, one of the most important things you'll have to do is come up with a name.

Top Ten Most Popular Baby Geek Names

Name: Bruce Wayne	Geekiness level: low
Name: Peter Parker	Geekiness level: low
Name: Selina Kyle	Geekiness level: low
Name: Stephanie Brown	Geekiness level: low
Name: Dick Grayson	Geekiness level: moderate
Name: Ramona Flowers	Geekiness level: moderate
Name: Leia Organa	Geekiness level: high
Name: Kakarot	Geekiness level: extremely high
Name: Kal-El	Geekiness level: bordering on dangerous
Name: Darth Vader	Geekiness level: maximum. Geekiness implosion imminent

Don't let anyone lie to you about having kids: once your little bundle of joy arrives, things are going to change. You're going to sleep and bathe less. You and your partner will probably spend far less time touching and more time cleaning up vomit. But seeing a new life blossom and grow into something amazing is, well, amazing. Though you will see the occasional couple whose kids are ugly, stupid, and/or mean (not yours, of course), most turn out to be little knowledge vacuums with a bright-eyed earnestness to match their eagerness to learn. It's at this age, when kids are absorbing knowledge like a black hole, that you can begin teaching them about the important things.

I'm not just talking about saying "thank you" or "sharing," I'm talking *important* stuff, like the difference between having a weapon which adds +haste or +crit, or why Android phones are far superior to iPhones (or vice-versa depending on which faction you belong to). Kids eat this kind of thing up and before you know it, you'll see them loving the same things you loved as a kid. They probably won't love *every*thing you did, though. Remember that your kids have a fragment of you in them but they are, at the same time, their own people with their own preferences. But regardless of your differences in tastes, there are some things that help bond geeks of all ages, rites of passages we all must undergo.

A father helps his son construct his first lightsaber.

Geek Rites of Passage

FIRST NERD RAGE. I remember my first nerd rage like it was yesterday. The year? 1997. The film? *Star Wars Episode IV: A New Hope* (Special Edition). Han Solo and Greedo were seated at the Mos Eisley cantina having a little chat. I braced myself for the moment of awesomeness when Han Solo, scoundrel that he is, shoots Greedo first as a pre-emptive counterattack. But that moment never came; instead, I couldn't believe my eyes as *Greedo,* not Han, shot first. What in the name of Yoda did I just see? This scene was so *wrong,* and there were these feelings bubbling up from deep inside me, feelings off ... *rage. Nerd rage.* It was an outrage I shared with my father and the two of us bonded over that moment in much the same way that countless other generations of geeks and nerds have bonded over similar geeky travesties.

FIRST CORRECTION ON A TECHNICAL DIFFERENCE. When your parents buy your child a Captain America action figure that turns out to actually be U.S. Agent (a similar, but entirely different, character) and he calls them out on it is a moment that will solidify your child's entry into the grand halls of geekdom.

> "Spock. This child is about to wipe out every living thing on Earth.
> Now, what do you suggest we do ... spank it?"
> — Dr. McCoy, *Star Trek: The Motion Picture*

THE FIRST TIME YOUR KIDS SEE A PIECE OF TECH GO OUT OF STYLE. Pencils and cassette tapes. To anyone born before 1990, the connection is obvious. Anyone born after, however, may have no idea what connects the two. That's because cassette tapes are outdated technology and have been for a long, long time. Such is the chain of technological development—new tech comes in, old tech goes out and becomes forgotten to all but the most nostalgic of technologists. When describing things like VHS tapes and CDs to your kids, they may respond with nothing more than a "Huh?" But as time goes on, they, too, will see the tech of their childhoods grow outdated and sent to pasture like a stallion past his prime.

THE FIRST TIME A MAJOR STUDIO PILLAGES YOUR CHILDHOOD LOOKING TO MAKE A QUICK BUCK. Remember my horrifying example from the previous chapter, the one about Michael Bay's *Doctor Who*? The soul-crushing disappointment and anger a geek feels when they see something they love warped into a twisted remnant of its former self is something we all must experience. Though these moments are painful, we do, eventually, get through them and realize that the things we loved weren't ruined because someone made a crass movie or TV show based on it. Yes, it's unfortunate, but the truth is that no one can take away your memories of enjoying the original thing in the first place.

THE FIRST TIME YOU EXPECT SOMETHING TO BE AWESOME AND IT TURNS OUT TO BE A PILE OF GARBAGE. "A live action Green Lantern movie? *Awesome!*" You remember those words? You said them, or if not you someone you know probably did. You dreamed about the day it would hit theaters. But then you went to the theater and saw the movie ... and your dreams were dispersed, sad, and unfulfilled. Broken expectations is another tenet of geek culture—it's our searing passion that makes things burn so bad when they're not any good. But it's this pain that bonds us, that unites us, that *drives* us to speak out against such ill-treatment of our favorite characters so that Hollywood (or whoever else) knows to do better when the inevitable re-boot comes around.

STAYING HOME TO DO SOMETHING GEEKY INSTEAD OF GOING OUT. While geeks are, in general, more sociable than the general public likes to believe, we're also a group who finds solace in solitude. Maybe your son's friends have called; they're getting together with some friends-of-friends

A well-decorated geek fridge.

at the noisy neighborhood hangout when his copy of the *Doctor Who 50th Anniversary* Blu-ray just came in. Or perhaps it's your daughter's high school's big game against their despised rivals and your entire school will be there ... except for her because she's not really into sports, and even if she was, she has a dungeon run in an MMO to attend. These are common dilemmas for the socially inclined geek to face. At times, it's best to suck it up and go do whatever less than desirable thing is being offered to you just to mix it up and get outside once in a while. (Although, sometimes it's perfectly fine to stay in and spend a quiet evening by yourself.)

CREATING YOUR FIRST PIECE OF FAN FICTION. For many geeks, creating works inspired by their favorite properties is a warm-up, a way of familiarizing themselves with the creative process while using a shell that is familiar to them. Many, *many* geeks do it, which is why so much of the internet is devoted to fan fiction/art.

FREAKING OUT OVER THE PREMATURE CANCELLATION OF A BELOVED SHOW. Television shows get cancelled. The ebb and flow of old shows flowing out and new shows flowing in helps keep original ideas coming in, as well as making sure shows don't overstay their welcome. But sometimes television shows don't get a chance to overstay their welcome; they don't get a chance at all. How many incredible shows, like *Firefly*, *Community*, or *My Mother the Car*, are never allowed to take off? The moment *Firefly* was cancelled, you had legions of geeks crying out all across the internet, protesting the premature removal of what was sure to be a sci-fi classic. This kind of thing is painfully tragic, but through this pain we, as geeks, are united, both within our own generation and across generations.

BUYING YOUR FIRST EXPENSIVE GEEK OBJECT. Fact: Geek toys, whether they're pewter figurines, cutting edge phones, or souped-up sports cars, get expensive. Fact: at some point or another, every geek will spend more money than they probably should on something geeky. Fact: I have a $100 Optimus Prime figure standing on my desk giving me a thumbs-up as I write this. Could that money have gone to something better, such as rent or diabetes medication for my badgers? Sure. But that's not the point. The point is that sometimes there are things so cool that it's our duty as geeks to buy it, consequences be *damned*.

> "Geeky people often have ... a mind with its own heartbeat."
> — Garret Freymann-Weyr, Printz Honor-winning author

The Future of Geekdom: Why It's a Good Day to Roll the Die

Something all geeks, young or old, skinny or heavy, socially awkward or loquaciously inclined, need to know is this: it's okay to be a geek. In fact, it's pretty great, and you should never listen to anyone who says otherwise.

The term "geek" dates back to 18th century Austria-Hungary, and stems from the word "gecken," meaning a circus freak who bites the heads off of live chickens. Needless to say, the concept of what a geek is has evolved over time, which goes to show how mutable and encompassing the term can be. Anyone who has passion for the things they love is a geek—it's the heart of what being a geek is about. Geeks come in all shapes and sizes, covering all subjects. When Matt Smith is discussing the techniques he uses when portraying the Eleventh Doctor? He's being an Acting Geek.[74] If your buddy the psych major can *not* shut up about how awesome the Stanford Prison Experiment was, he's being a Psychology Geek. If your local preacher knows the Bible inside and out ... yeah, he's a Bible Geek.

Geekery truly knows no bounds. Anyone who doesn't have something they geek out over is, honestly, kind of sad. These are people devoid of zeal; they're zombies wandering around without the fire of life burning inside. So tell your kids to *never* be ashamed of the things they like. Yes, they may get picked on. Or they may not. Either way, you'll be there to help them embrace their interests and not give a damn about what those other folks are saying, and wear that badge of geekiness with pride.

Calling someone a geek used to be an insult—it implied someone who was introverted and weird. Well, it's a new millennium, has been for a while. The meaning of the word has changed, as has the diverse number of things people geek out about. Anyone who has fire in their gut and determination in their eyes, anyone who has ever stayed up late into the night working on a project or goofing off online, anyone who has ever done *anything* worth caring about—they're all geeks. So if someone tells you that you're a bit of a geek, you look them right in the eye and you thank them. Because it's a geek's world. Everyone else is just taking up space.

---

[74] And also kind of a Sci-Fi Geek. Geek types aren't mutually exclusive, people.

Index

30 Rock, 205
101 Dalmatians, 220

Aensland, Morrigan, 195
Aeowyn, 226
Akroyd, Dan, 15
Agent Smith, 149
Alien, 207
Aliens, 200, 207
Allen, Barry, 227
Amazing Superpowers, 93
Angelou, Maya, 206
Angry Birds, 118
Animal House, 135
Anime geek, 25
Aqua Teen Hunger Force, 31
Aragorn, 226
Aran, Samus, 210
Archimedes, 11
Arm Fall Off Boy, 101
Arrested Development, 214
Arwyn, 226
Asbestos Lady, The, 105
Austen, Chuck, 95
Autobot, 151
Automotive geek, 24
Axe Cop, 92

Babylon 5, 52
Bachelor/bachelorette parties, 222-223
Back to the Future, 82-83
Barry, Dave, 123
Batman, 86, 87, 95, 148, 166, 168, 176, 206, 227
Batman & Robin, 15
Batman: Animated Series: The, 211
Batmanghelidjh, Camila, 206
Battlefield Earth, 50
Battlestar Galactica, 52, 55, 219
Bayonetta, 39
Bayside High School, 143, 218
Bejeweled, 118
Benson, Amber, 199
Bezos, Jeff, 126
Bieber, Justin, 44
Big Bang Theory, The, 8, 153, 166, 203
Big Brother, 156
Birdemic, 68
Black Canary, 227
Blade Runner, 19, 20
Blazers, 32
Book of Biff, 91
Bouncing Boy, 99-100

Bowties, 31
Brawl in the Family, 90
Buffy the Vampire Slayer, 205, 208
Burton, Levar, 192

C-3PO, 224
Cabin in the Woods, 52
Calculator watches, 30
Campbell, Bruce, 192
Captain America, 196, 231
Carey, Mariah, 52
Catwoman, 38, 227
Caveman, 86
Chainsawsuit, 93
Chicago Bears, 20
Child, Julia, 179
Child's Play, 176
Clash of the Geeks, 176
Clean-shaven face, 32
Cobain, Kurt, 30
College of William and Mary, The, 140
Cologne/perfume, 32
Color Kid, 103
Comic book geek, 22
Community, 234
Connor, Sarah, 200, 209
Consumer Electronics Show, 189-190
Cookie Monster, 52
Cooking, 178-185
Cooper, Sheldon, 153, 166
Corpses Are Forever, 70
Cosplay, 31, 194-196
Countdown to Final Crisis, 95-96
Coupling, 59
Course of the Force, 175
Creative Commons, 177
Crocs, 30
Cry for Justice, 98-99
Curie, Marie, 13
Cyclops, 225

Da Vinci, Leonardo, 12
Dante, 195
Darkstalkers, 195
Darth Vader, 51, 224
Date Night, 205
Day, Felicia, 65, 201-202, 205
DC Comics, 22, 95-99, 176
Deliverance, 83
Denmead, Ken, 9
Devil May Cry 3, 195
Diablo III, 23, 217
Diesel, Vin, 72
Discworld, 80

Dog Welder, 107
Donors Choose, 176-177
Dr. McCoy, 232
Dr. Who, 31, 50
Dr. Who, 8, 20, 86, 87, 124, 217-218, 232
"Dueling Banjos," 83
Dungeons and Dragons, 18, 53, 71-77, 93, 110, 189, 201, 219

Edgerton, Winifred, 12
Edison, Thomas, 12, 13, 14
Einstein, Albert, 213
Electronic Entertainment Expo, 189
Elfman, Danny, 225
Empire Strikes Back, The, 167
Escape From New York, 83
Evil Dead, 198

Faber College, 142
Facebook, 124
Family Ties, 140
Fan fiction, 220-221
Fedoras, 31
Fellowship of the Ring, The, 82, 226
Fetishes, 219-222
Fett, Boba, 149
Fey, Tina, 200, 205
Fifth Element, The, 213
Fillion, Nathan, 19
Final Fantasy VII, 38
Final Fantasy Tactics, 118, 149
Firefly, 45, 220, 234
Fitocracy, 113
Flash, The, 227
Flat Hat Club, The, 140
Food geek, 26
Ford, Harrison, 19
Forks High School, 143
Fox, Charles, 227
Freymann-Weyr, Garret, 235
Fresh Prince of Bel-Air, The, 56
Frodo, 226
Fund Science, 177
Furries, 219-220

Gabrielle, 209
Gambit, 226
Game of Thrones, A, 80, 81, 168
Gamer geek, 23
Gandalf, 226
Gates, Bill, 27, 175
Gellar, Sarah Michelle, 208
Gen Con, 189

Ghostbusters, 15
GI Joe, 154
Gibson, Mel, 19
Gilligan's Island, 154
Gimbel, Norman, 227
Glau, Summer, 109
Glitter, 52
Glover, Danny, 19
Golden Eye, 67
Golden Eye 64, 67
Golden Girls, 53
Goodall, Jane, 206
Greedo, 231
Green Bay Packers, 20
Green, John, 199
Green Lantern, 98, 227, 232
Greendale Community College, 141
Grey, Jean, 225
Gridiron Secret Society, 140
Grooming, 33-34
Gruber, Hans, 36
Guild, The, 205
Gunnerkrigg Court, 92
Gunshow, 94
Gunstringer, The, 111
Gygax, Ernest Gary, 77

Halo, 66-67, 113
Hairstyles, 35-41
Hamilton, Linda, 200, 209
Hangover, The, 222
Hard Rock Zombies, 64
Hardwick, Chris, 115, 201
Hark, A Vagrant, 94
Harry Potter, 206
Heady, Lena, 209
Heder, Jon, 29
Hentai, 220
Hercules, Legendary Journeys, The, 209
Heroes Reborn, 96
History geek, 19
Hitler, Adolph, 15
Hobbit: An Unexpected Journey, The, 82
Hofstadter, Leonard, 153, 166
Hogwarts, 141
Hudson, Ernie, 15
Humans vs. Zombies, 110-111
Hunger Games, 55

I Am Legend, 83
Imperial March, 224
Incredible Hulk, The, 32, 149
Incredible Hulk, The, 22
Incredibles, The, 86
Internet, 122-133

Iron Chef, 12
Iron Man, 31
Iron Man: The Crossing, 96

Jackman, Hugh, 22, 195
Jackson, Peter, 82
Jackson, Samuel, 201
Jackson, Shirley Ann, 200
Jersey Shore, 24, 177
Jetpack Joyride, 118
Johnson, Marguerite, Ann, 206
Joker, 95, 227
Jordan, Hal, 227
Jovovich, Milla, 160
Juwanna Mann, 83

Kando, Koji, 225
Kinect, 111
Klingons, 56, 149
Knotts, Don, 15

LaBeouf, Shia, 217
Lackadaisy, 92
Lagan, Gurren, 195-196
Large Hadron Collider, 15, 149
Laser Tag, 113
Lawless, Lucy, 209
Leaf and Niggle, 82
Leather jackets, 32
Lee, Stan, 85
Legend of Zelda, 149
Legend of Zelda: Skyward Sword, 111
Let's Be Friends Again, 91
Leverage, 59
Levy, Shuki, 226
Lion King, The, 220
Littner, Yoko, 195-196
Live Action Role Playing, 71, 110, 218
Locke, John, 149
Long Kiss Goodnight, The, 201
Lord of the Rings, The, 82, 168, 226-227
Lost, 8, 149
Lt. Worf, 181
Lucas, George, 89
Lumiere, Louis, 12

Maathai, Wangari, 206
Mad Max, 83
Mad Men, 31
Madagascar, 220
Magic: The Gathering, 71, 189
Manga, 25
Manly Guys Doing Manly Things, 91
Manos: The Hands of Fate, 68
Mario, 66, 224

Mario Kart, 51, 66
Mario Kart 64, 139
Mario Party, 66
Marston, William Moulton, 207
Martin, George R. R., 80, 81
Marvel, 22, 95-99
Marvel Girl, 225
Mary Sue, 88
Matrix, The, 149, 150
Matter Eater Lad, 100
Mayans, 15
Mean Girls, 200, 205
Megamind, 86, 205
Ménage à 3, 93
Metroid, 210
Mighty Morphin' Power Rangers, 170
Milne, A.A., 119
Mjolnir, 151
MODAK, 104, 105
MODAM, 104-105
Monster Camp, 218
Moon, Sailor, 151
Morpheus, 150
Motion gaming systems, 112
Mr. Rogers, 50
Murray, Bill, 15, 46
Music geek, 21
Mutton chops, 30
My Mother the Car, 234
Mystery Science Theater 3000, 67, 196

Nail polish, 32
NASCAR, 45
Neckbeards, 30
Neckbears, 30
Neo, 150, 166
Nichols, Nichelle, 200
Ninja Terminator, 70

O'Connor, Renée, 209
Oglaf, 91
Optimus Prime, 151, 167, 197
Order of Angell, 140
Order of the Stick, 93

Parker, Peter, 149
Parody porn, 220
Paste-Pot Pete, 104
Paul, Adrian, 31
Pegg, Simon, 27
Penny Arcade, 90, 149, 189
Penny Arcade Expo, 189
Perry Fellow Bibleship, 93
Pets, 166-170
Phoenix, 225
Pikachu, 66

Pirates of the Caribbean, The, 59
Plan 9 from Outer Space, 67
Planet of the Apes, 83
Plants vs. Zombies, 118
Playstation Motion, 111
Ponytails, 31
Pratchett, Terry, 80, 109
Princess Leia, 224
Princess Peach, 224
Professor Xavier, 41, 226
Professor Xavier's School for Gifted
Youngsters, 142, 226
Pryde of the X-Men, 226
PVP, 92

R2-D2, 224
Ramis, Harold, 15
Reading body language, 46-50
Retro clothes, 31
Return of the King, The, 82
Revenge of the Ninja, 68
Ring, The, 83
Ripley, Ellen, 200, 207
Road Goes Ever On, The, 226
Robin, 227
RoboCop, 149
Rock-afire Explosion, The, 218
Roddenberry, Gene, 88
Rogue, 37
Room, The, 43, 68
Rowling, J.K., 206
Run for Your Lives Marathon, 112
Russell, Kurt, 172

San Diego Comic-Con, 31, 109, 190,
205
Sarah Connor Chronicles, The, 86
Saturday Morning Breakfast Cereal, 93
Saturday Night Live, 205
Saved By the Bell, 218
Saw, 222
Scalzi, John, 176
Sci-fi geek, 19
Scrabble, 218
Screech, 218
Scroll and Key, 141
Seagal, Steven, 31
Sega, 221
Segal, Stephen H., 229
Servo, Tom, 196
Shore, Howard, 226
Simpson, Homer, 135
Simpson, Marge, 135
Sixth Sense, The, 51
Smith, Paula, 88
Smith, Will, 56

Socks and sandals, 30
Solo, Han, 150, 224, 231
Song of Fire and Ice, A, 81
Sonic the Hedgehog, 221
South Harmon Institute of Technology,
142
Spider-Man, 23, 86, 87, 88, 95, 151
Spider-Man, 15
Spider-Man: One More Day, 98
Spider-Man: The Clone Saga, 96
Sports geek, 20
Squirrel Girl, 102
Stackhouse, Jason, 31
Stallone, Sylvester, 172
Star Trek, 20, 46, 88, 148, 200
Star Trek: The Next Generation, 192
Star Wars, 19, 20, 52, 89-90, 224, 231
Starcraft 2, 45, 147, 229
Stark, Tony, 36, 96
Steampunk, 31
Stinson, Barney, 33
Stop or My Mom Will Shoot, 172
Street Fighter, 70, 202
Strife, Cloud, 38
Stross, Charles, 129
Summers, Buffy, 200
Super Mario Bros, 170,
Super Mario Cart, 66
Super Nintendo, 66
Super Smash Bros., 66, 194
Superboy, 227
Superdog, 168, 169
Superman, 86-87, 151, 167, 176, 227
Swamp Thing, 227
Swanson, Kristy, 208
Sweatpants, 31

Tabletop geek, 15
Tech geek, 27
Terminator: Sarah Connor Chronicles,
The, 209
Terminator, The, 83, 86, 209
Terminator 2: Judgment Day, 83, 86,
200
Terminator 3, 86
Tesla, Nikola, 12, 13, 14
Texas A & M, 140
Thing, The, 172
Thor, 151
Three Word Phase, 94
Timm, Bruce, 211
Tolkien, J.R.R., 82, 187
Toulouse, Stephen, 176
Transformers, 167
Trekkie, 88
"Trekkie's Tale, A," 88

Troll 2, 69
Twilight, 190
Twitter, 124
Two Towers, The, 82
Typhoid Mary, 15
Tyson, Neil deGrasse, 15

Ultimatum, 99
University of California-Sunnydale, 141
University of Georgia, 140
University of Michigan, 140
Utilikilts, 30

Valente, Catherynne M., 176

Walsh, Rob, 226
Warhammer, 18, 71
Washburn, Margaret Floy, 200
Wasserman, Ron, 226
Wayne, Bruce, 211
We Can Be Heroes, 176
Weaver, Sigourney, 200
Webcomics, 90-94
Wedding themes, 224-227
Weebler, Ernest, 172
Wheaton, Wil, 43, 176
Wii, 111
Wikipedia, 177
William McKinley High School, 143
Williams, John, 224, 227
Willis, Bruce, 51, 213
Winfrey, Oprah, 205-206
Whedon, Joss, 208
Wolverine, 35, 225
Wonder Twin Zan, 106
Wonder Woman, 176, 194, 207, 210,
227
Word Wars, 218
World 1-1 (Above Ground Theme), 225
World of Warcraft, 49, 139

X-Men, 22, 95, 173, 225-226
X-Men Animated Series Theme, 226
X-Men Origins: Wolverine, 195
Xena, 209
Xena: Warrior Princess, 209

Yale, 141
Yankovic, Al, 30
Yothers, Tina, 140
Yu-Gi-Oh, 156

Zatanna, 227
Zombies, 15, 154-160

About the author

Alex Langley can control gravity, swim at over eight-hundred miles per second, and has a dangerous, borderline nuclear passion for writing. He also writes news, interviews, and comics for the website rocketllama.com, has over 14,000 followers on twitter, and edits content for geek girl/web celebrity @actionchick Katrina Hill at actionflickchick.com. Thousands follow his work online, and he has been a speaker on panels at conventions, including Wonder-Con, and San Diego Comic-Con International. His published works also include academic papers.

Marko Head

About the illustrator

Nick Langley is a fan of comic books and tabletop gaming. He is a BFA Graphic Design graduate and cartoonist for Rocket Llama World Headquarters (rocketllama.com), the Action Flick Chick (actionchick.com), and Live And Let Dice (liveandletdice.com). He is also the founder of the Workday Comic (workdaycomic.com), a project inspired by Scott McCloud (*Zot!*, *Understanding Comics*) and Steve Bisette's (*Swamp Thing*, *Taboo*) 24-Hour Comics, and through it has collaborated on with many artists, including David Mack (*Kabuki*, *Daredevil*).

ARE YOU A 'MOVIE FREAK'?

"I'LL BE BACK."
– THE TERMINATOR, THE TERMINATOR (1984)

To the movies, that is. And so will you with the help of *Sci-Fi Movie Freak*, a celebration of some of the greatest science-fiction movies of all time. Your inner geek will freak finding everything from classics like *Metropolis*, *Forbidden Planet*, a 2001: A Space Odyssey to modern movies including *Avatar*, *Moon*, and *Inception*, and even the entertaining "failures" *Robot Monster*, *Gammera the Invincible*, and *Battlefield Ea*

ITEM# W5966 • $21.99

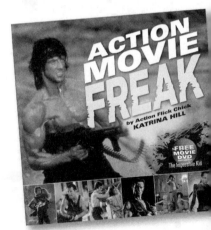

Written by woman of action Katrina "Action Flick Chick" Hill, *Action Movie Freak* is packed with spine-tingling excitement and thrilling moments that make action movies a beloved genre for those who crave crashing cars, exploding buildings, and faces getting kicked six ways to Sunday. With badass heroes that ain't got time to bleed, women warriors, thrilling chases and outrageous fisticuffs, *Action Movie Freak* celebrates a wide variety of more than 100 movies that have left audiences on the edge of their seats.

ITEM# V8194 • $22.99